The Mankato Reconcilliation Powwow

The Mankato Reconcilliation Powwow

Loren Dean Boutin

North Star Press of St. Cloud, Inc.
St. Cloud, Minnesota

Printed in the United States
by Sentinel Printing, St. Cloud, Minnesota

Published by
North Star Press of St. Cloud, Inc.
P.O. Box 451
St. Cloud, Minnesota 56302

Table of Contents

Preface vii

Chapter 1:   The Beginning 1

Chapter 2:   Events That Lead to the Powwow 10

Chapter 3:   The First Reconciliation Powwow 21

Chapter 4:   Getting Organized 29

Chapter 5:   Spin-offs from the Powwow 39

Chapter 6:   Mahkato Education Day Project 53

Chapter 7:   Integral Parts of the Powwow 65

Chapter 8:   Ceremonies at the Powwow 76

Chapter 9:   Vendors 89

Chapter 10:   The Spectators 92

Chapter 11:   Spiritual Experiences 95

Epilogue 111

Summary of Historical Events 118

References 120

Index 121

Preface

A T THE 2010 POWWOW IN MANKATO, Minnesota, the thirty-eighth, some unusual things happened. Several of the people providing leadership for holding the powwow announced that they would be retiring after this one. These included: Ray Owen, the spiritual leader; Leonard Wabasha, the president of the Mdewakanton Association; and Bob Rolfes, who has been treasurer of the club, later referred to as the association, for many years. The impetus for it all appeared to be that this was the thirty-eighth powwow. With this one, there has been a powwow for each of the thirty-eight American Indians hanged in Mankato in 1862. There was a note of finality about that, although there also was talk of the next year's powwow and there were already some preparations being made for it.

During this powwow the two surviving founders of the powwow (Bud Lawrence and Jim Buckley) met with me to ask if I would write the history of the powwow. My response was that I was honored to be asked to do that, and I gladly accepted the assignment. I told them I would get started on it right away, and they seemed pleased with my enthusiasm, both of them expressing confidence that I would do a fine job and thanking me for my willingness to take it on. We all knew at once that the writing of this book would be a major undertaking because the Mankato Powwow is more than an ordinary powwow. It is certainly an extraordinary powwow. What makes it special is the way it began, where it is held, and the reasons for it.

I spent much of the next two days of the powwow talking with many of the long-standing members of the powwow committee, taking pictures of them, and taking pictures of the powwow itself to include in my history book. I snapped shots of many of the dancers in their varieties of elaborate and colorful regalia, the many vending concessions, the dances, the ceremonies, the drums, and the powwow officials. I was trying to capture in these pictures some of the essence of the powwow, but that effort was mostly futile. After the powwow had concluded and all the dancers, drummers, vendors, and spectators and everyone else had departed for their homes, I realized that the essence of the powwow cannot be captured in pictures. And for some important parts of the powwow, pictures weren't even allowed. Much more than pictures is needed to really get a good perspective on the powwow. I began to realize the importance of the history of it, the reasons for it, and how it all happened.

The Mankato Powwow is referred to as a "reconciliation powwow." This description says a lot, but unless the history of the powwow is known, it doesn't mean very much by itself. In this case, "reconciliation" means the repair of the relationships between the local white community and the indigenous American Indian communities exiled from the local area after a bitter war between these communities. The war was called "The 1862 Sioux Uprising." It resulted in an estimated 500 to 1,000 settlers killed by the American Indians, scores of white soldiers killed, many Dakota warriors killed, and (on December 26, 1862) thirty-eight of the Dakota warriors hanged simultaneously. That hanging was and is the largest simultaneous execution ever to have taken place in the entire history of the United States, or perhaps even the largest in the history of the whole world. That hanging happened in downtown Mankato. And, in addition, the local white communities were so full of hate for the Dakota that they wanted to be rid of all of them, once and for all. To this end, they actually captured all who could be found and forcefully exiled them to distant places.

After all of that horror, the relationship between the white communities in southern Minnesota and the Dakota remained estranged and festering for more than a hundred and ten years. Those Dakota who remained in this area were often treated like animals. For many years the white population could legally shoot American Indians on sight and then be rewarded for having done that. When a soldier's pay for a month of service was ten dollars, and the cost of a horse was twenty dollars, the collectable bounty for an Indian scalp was seventy-five dollars. It is not surprising, therefore, that any local American Indians who escaped being exiled either left the area, hid themselves, or denied their Indian ancestry in order to protect themselves and avoid being killed. There are verified accounts of people being killed when they merely looked like American Indians. Consequently, until after World War II, and the Korean War, and the war in Vietnam (in all of which the American Indians distinguished themselves for their military service), most American Indians avoided passing through the Mankato and New Ulm areas like avoiding the plague. They did not feel welcome or safe in these areas. They either passed quickly through these areas at night or they went out of their way to skirt these places entirely. The Mankato Powwow was initiated to bring the American Indians back to these areas, and it did ultimately begin the healing of the awfully wounded relationships between the Dakota and white communities.

Now there are monuments and plaques in downtown Mankato commemorating the Dakota warriors hanged and the war that cost so many lives. The Dakota American Indians now come to these areas without fear, while proudly proclaiming their heritage. A local school is named after them. They are invited to talk to school children about their culture, and they do that in an educational effort to dispel any misinformation about them and their heritage. The Dakota have returned to live as members of the general community, and they can do this with the confidence that they are accepted by the local communities.

Most of the content of this book is based upon the personal observations of the author or upon personal communications with Bud Lawrence, Jim Buckley, Ray Owen, and other prominent participants and associates of the Mankato Powwow. Much of this information is new, never before having appeared in print, such as the many stories told to me by my "consultants." It is my own perspective that no apology is necessary for the lack of an extensive bibliography or list of references from which information was obtained, because not much of the content of this book was obtained from printed sources other than those few listed in the bibliography. All of this is in keeping with the fact that American Indian history has traditionally been handed down orally.

Chapter One

The Beginning

THERE IS A VERY BEAUTIFUL PLACE at the bend in the Minnesota River where the cities of Mankato and North Mankato are now located. Here the Minnesota River begins to flow in a northerly direction to join the Mississippi River at Fort Snelling. At this bend in the river is the confluence of the Blue Earth River with the Minnesota River. Surrounding cities have now designated this area as park lands because of its beauty, and the park lands are very special to the local communities. But this place has always been special to the American Indians. Before the white man came, the American Indians held annual powwows there.

In this context, "powwow" is defined as a conference among North American Indians. For the American Indians, a powwow served many purposes. American Indians of many tribes would come from hundreds of miles around to meet at this place, to trade with one another, to celebrate whatever needed celebrating, to dress in their finest beaded buckskins and feathered dancing regalia and sing and dance to their drumming, and to hold a variety of ceremonies. There were ceremonies for naming, honoring, and marrying. There were give-away ceremonies. And there was feasting. Even some of the feasts were ceremonies in remembrance of someone. And there was storytelling over campfires. American Indian spirituality flourished. Even the spirits attended the powwows. These powwows lasted for several days or even weeks, and they were held annually for hundreds of years.

The American Indians began to have problems when white men invaded their homelands hundreds of years ago. It all began in 1492 when the first white men arrived on the East Coast. Relationships between the whites and the American Indians were friendly at first, with the American Indians helping the white people to learn how to get food and otherwise survive in this new environment. But conflicts developed when more and more whites arrived to develop settlements and take over large areas of land for farming, depriving the American Indians of their land. The American Indians had no concept of ownership of land and they ceded their traditional hunting grounds to the whites with great reluctance. The land had always been available to the American Indians, but now the whites were claiming exclusive ownership and depriving the American Indians of their hunting grounds. The conflicts that resulted sometimes turned into horrible wars, which the American Indians invariably lost even though they were the victors in many of the battles. The incursions of whites in the East forced the American Indians to move west into the homelands of other American Indians of different tribes and nations. This resulted in the American Indians fighting among themselves for territory.

As the white man continued to move westward, a domino effect developed. The whites pushed the American Indians, the American Indians pushed other American Indians, and ultimately the fighting reached the Minnesota Territory and beyond. For decades, the Ojibwe (Chippewa) and the Dakota were at war with one another. As a result of all of this conflict, the American Indians suffered in many ways. In addition to the casualties the American Indians sustained in their fights with each other, there were huge numbers of casualties from their wars with the white men, and they were ravaged by the white man's diseases from which they had no immunity and for which they had no defense. The total population of American Indians was diminished from an estimated 125 million before the white man arrived to less than 250,000 in the U.S. Census of 1882.[1] It was all a result of the white man's western "progress."

By 1862 the powwows at the bend in the river had not been held for many years. The American Indians and the powwows had been displaced by the territorial advances of the white man. And in 1862 the peaceful existence that the American Indians had known for hundreds of years in southern Minnesota came to an abrupt end. The American Indians in this area had suffered as much deprivation, victimization, and abuse at the hands of some corrupt white people as they could tolerate. They had been promised a life of ease and plenty in exchange for their lands, but these promises were not kept. The Dakota were now hungry and on the brink of starvation with their traditional ways of providing for themselves taken from them.

On August 18, 1862, the Dakota entered into a desperate war with the whites to take back the lands taken from them and to reestablish their old ways in which they were not dependent on the white man for anything. They killed many of the settlers who had established homesteads on what the American Indians considered to be their hunting grounds. They attacked the City of New Ulm twice and Fort

Ridgely twice, and there were several other major engagements in this war, but the war ended in only six weeks with the Dakota having suffered a devastating defeat.

The Dakota had won almost every battle of the war, but they lost the war itself because of the overwhelming numbers of white men. Even before the war began, Chief Little Crow had tried to warn his warriors, telling them that for each white man killed ten would come to take his place. Little Crow was opposed to going to war with the whites, but he had been unable to dissuade his people from going to war. After their defeat, the Dakota were almost totally exiled from southern Minnesota and deported to distant places, forcefully relocated to some desolate lands in Nebraska and South Dakota.

When the war ended, the United States Army punished the Dakota by hanging thirty-eight of the warriors who had participated in the war. The Army had sentenced 303 warriors to be hanged, every warrior they could find who had participated in the war. But in the middle of the Civil War, when he must have been very busy with other things, President Abraham Lincoln still took the time necessary to intervene and would not allow the Army to hang that many. In anticipation of hanging hundreds of American Indians, the Army had built a scaffold capable of hanging forty at a time. Apparently, they had no desire to spend the whole winter hanging 303 American Indians one or two or even several at a time. Forty at a time would get the job done quickly. In the end, President Lincoln said that they could hang only the worst forty. When that list was established, he himself

Sketch of the hanging appeared in *Harper's Weekly* magazine following the hanging.

commuted the death sentence of one of those. On the morning when the hanging was to happen, one more of the initial forty was found innocent of what had been charged against him. Consequently, thirty-eight warriors were actually hanged in downtown Mankato in what was, nevertheless, the largest simultaneous execution ever to take place in the entire history of the United States.

Fourteen hundred soldiers and an estimated five to six thousand civilian spectators were present at the hanging. People came from hundreds of miles away to witness this gruesome spectacle.

When the hanging was over, the bodies were loaded in wagons and taken to be buried in a shallow mass grave on the sandy river bottom nearby. During their first night in the ground, the bodies were dug up and stolen from the grave to be sold and used as cadavers for medical study. Consequently, today there is no grave for the warriors who were hanged. And nobody now knows even the exact location where the gravesite had been located. Furthermore, nobody knows what ultimately happened to any of the bodies except one. That was the body of Cut Nose, one of the leaders of the Dakota in the war. His body was dissected by W.W. Mayo, the father of the famous Mayo brothers, and his skeleton continued to hang in Mayo Clinic for another 150 years. Most of it is still there.[2]

The bulk of the three hundred Dakota warriors condemned to hang but not hanged were sent to prison in Iowa. All the remaining Dakota, men, women, and children, whether or not they participated in the war, were rounded up and eventually shipped to Nebraska and South Dakota. The white population remained leery of American Indians for a long time after all the Dakota were exiled and banished from the area. There still remained the tribe of 2,000 Winnebagos located just a few miles South of Mankato and, although they had not participated in the 1862 War, the Winnebagos were known to be friendly with the Dakota.

KNIGHTS OF THE FOREST

THE KNIGHTS OF THE FOREST was a very secret organization started by three businessmen in 1863 in Mankato. It had as its purpose the elimination of all the American Indians from the State of Minnesota, especially the Winnebagos. It boasted of as many as fifty members comprised mostly of Mankato businessmen. The main purpose and focus of the organization was to force the Winnebagos or Hochunks south of Mankato to leave Minnesota completely.[3] At the end of the 1862 War with the Dakotas, the hanging of thirty-eight Dakota warriors in

Mankato, and the exile to distant places of every other Dakota that could be found (with very few exceptions), the general population of citizens in the area was so traumatized by the slaughter of settlers during the war that for a long time they continued to believe all American Indians were hostile. They could not believe they were safe until all American Indians were removed from the area. To complete the elimination of American Indians in the area, the Knights of the Forest wanted to be rid of the Winnebagos.

Because the Winnebagos were known to be friendly with the Dakota, it was believed they would have participated in the war if the Dakota had been successful in their assaults on Fort Ridgely and New Ulm. In that case, it was believed, there would have followed an assault on Mankato by the Dakota from the west, and the Winnebagos from the east and south. If that had happened, Mankato likely would have fallen in a blood bath. Local white communities feared and distrusted the Winnebagos. In addition, and perhaps of equal or even more importance, the Winnebago reservation was sitting on about 250 square miles of the best, most fertile farmland in the whole world. The elimination of the Winnebagos would not only help the whites feel less fearful, but also would have the additional advantage of making that premium land available to white settlers.

THE SCALPING LAWS

THE IMAGE OF INDIAN SAVAGES scalping innocent white people, women and children included, has been imbedded in the minds of the non-Indian population for a very long time. This image has been given to school children in history clases taught in our schools. It is still being taught there. It's also the image conveyed in movies that emerge from Hollywood. But the whole truth is that scalping is an invention of white men and was practiced in Europe before white men came to America. The American Indians have been much more the victims of scalping than the perpetrators of this gruesome practice.

The taking of scalps evolved as a more practical way of proving a body count after a battle in a war.[4] Previously, heads were lopped off and gathered for proof of the number killed. If a large number of the enemy were killed, this practice was cumbersome. Cutting off a good-sized piece of scalp from the top of the head was much more expedient.

The way the American Indians were victimized by scalping was by white men putting a bounty on the scalps of American Indians as part of their concerted efforts to rid the country of American Indians once and for all.[5] The government started by paying American Indians to scalp their enemies in the wars they were having, notably the English and the French. Then they paid the American Indians to scalp other American Indians, paying the most for the scalp of an adult male Indian, less for the scalp of a female, and still less for the scalp of a child. All the while, white men collected these bounties too, and some of them made a business out of it. White men would go out in hunting parties, shooting and killing American Indians for their scalps to collect the bounty. All of the original thirteen colonies had scalping laws, according to written accounts.[6] The amount of payment for an adult male Indian scalp in colonial days amounted to one hundred pounds of silver, four times the average annual income for a farmer at the time. In a relatively short time, it was difficult to find any American Indians in the East, but (according to Churchill),[7] "scalp bounty [laws] were enacted in every state and territory" as the whites continued their incursions into the Indian territories of the West. Scalp bounty laws authorized the killing of hostile American Indians, collecting the scalps, and then being monetarily rewarded for that.

A scalping law was initially assumed to exist in the State of Minnesota in 1863. It provided a payment of seventy-five dollars to the farmer who shot Chief Little Crow in 1863. Little Crow was picking wild berries northwest of Hutchinson when a farmer shot him with no provocation, apparently for the scalp bounty. Later, when the body was discovered to be that of Little Crow, the payment was increased to $500. But in actuality, there was no law that authorized this killing, and, in fact, Little Crow was murdered.[8] The circumstances of Little Crow's killing at that time satisfied the legal requirements for a charge of murder against the farmer who shot him, but instead the farmer was lauded as a hero and rewarded for his "great service to the State of Minnesota." Blue Earth County, where the Mankato Powwow is held, did have its own scalping law for a short time, authorizing a payment of twenty-five dollars (later increased to $200) for a scalp of a hostile American Indian. This was in 1863, just after the 1862 War, when all the settlers were still panicked about American Indians and all American Indians were thought to be hostile. However, incredibly, it is reported that the county never had to pay the bounty. What makes that so unbelievable is the fact that the "Knights of the Forest" was gunning for any kind of Indian.

It is reported that in 1863 the members of the Knights of the Forest would station themselves near and outside the borders of the Winnebago Reservation near Mankato and ambush and kill any Indian who wandered outside or crossed the border.[9] There is no available information about how many American Indians were killed in this way, and the records of the Knights of the Forest Society were lost in a fire.

Despite the secrecy of the Knights of the Forest Society, it is likely that government officials learned of the society and its activities. Thomas Hughes, perhaps the most credible historian for the Mankato area, stated, "Through the work of this society and the persistent clamor of the people all over the state, Congress was finally induced during February and March 1863, to pass acts for the removal of both tribes [the Dakota and the Winnebago] from Minnesota to Nebraska and South Dakota."[10] The society is thought to have been at least partially responsible for the government's removal of the 2,000 Winnebagos to Crow Creek in Nebraska in May of 1863.[11]

For the local citizenry around Mankato, 1863 was an opportune time to take aim at the Winnebagos because new ordinances had been enacted that provided a reward in the form of a bounty for Indian scalps. There was an order by an adjutant general of the Minnesota militia authorizing payment of twenty-five dollars to military scouts for the scalp of a hostile Indian.[12] Peculiarly, this order extended to civilians also, who would be paid seventy-five dollars for Indian scalps. (In this context, all American Indians were thought to be hostile.) The order was issued on July 4th, just after the shooting of Little Crow. In September 1863, the governor of Minnesota raised the bounty for an Indian scalp to $200 "to increase the number of such 'Independent Scouts' [referring to civilians who shoot American Indians] and to multiply that of dead American Indians shot on sight."[13] Records indicate that the Minnesota militia actually paid some scalp bounties, though the number appears to be five or less.

For a short period of time, Blue Earth County also had its own separate bounty ordinance, briefly mentioned above. This was a law actually enacted by the local government, which provided a bounty of twenty-five dollars for an Indian scalp, but it is reported that the county never had to pay that bounty. Two years later, in 1865, the Blue Earth County bounty for an Indian scalp was also raised to $200, but by that time there were no American Indians to be found in the area.

The white man's animosity toward American Indians continued to be evident in the Mankato-New Ulm area for many, many decades. For example, in 1912 a granite monument was placed on the location of the hanging of the thirty-eight in Mankato. It was much like a tombstone, about four feet high, three feet wide, and about a foot thick, set upright upon another piece of granite about the same size lying flat on the ground, the combination of stones weighing about 8,500 pounds. This monument was designed to be neither positive nor negative in its

This monument was located at the site of the hanging near the intersection of Front and Main Streets in downtown Mankato. (Picture courtesy of Blue Earth County Historical Society)

message. It was not intended to honor the hanged Dakota, nor was it intended to be any kind of ill-advised boast about having hanged them. It was merely a statement of fact.

One would think that this marker would not be cause for or engender much protest, but it did rankle quite a few people. Some thought it was honoring the thirty-eight Dakota hanged. It stimulated such questions as, "Why should they be honored?" and "What did they do that was honorable?" and "Shouldn't we honor instead the hundreds of settlers they killed?" Others seemed to think that indeed it was some kind of boast about having hanged the Dakota. Clarence Darrow, the famous lawyer, visited Mankato in 1937 and is reported to have expressed disgust at seeing the monument. He is quoted in the *Mankato Free Press* on December 27, 1937, as having said, "I can't make myself believe that the people of a civilized community would want to commemorate such an atrocious crime. I would never believe it if I didn't see the marker with my own eyes." It is not clear that he even knew about the subsequent grave robbery.

That simple marker, as neutral in its message as it was, was the object of much controversy and even much abuse. The marker was sometimes vandalized by having red paint thrown on it. It looked quite gory splashed with red paint. A former editor of the Mankato Free Press, Ken Berg, was generally in favor of reconciling with the American Indians, but he wrote many editorials protesting the recognition given to the Dakota warriors while their victims, the slain settlers, were relatively forgotten, at least from his perspective. Consequently, the Dakota continued to stay away from the Mankato and New Ulm communities and would go out of their way to avoid the area when traveling through southern Minnesota. The monument, together with the editorials, seemed to refresh the long-standing antagonism between the whites and the American Indians.

The monument was removed by the City of Mankato in 1971 and buried under a sand pile in a city storage lot. Subsequently, it disappeared quite mysteriously. That monument was comprised of two pieces of solid granite which would not have been easy to move, but apparently it had enough negativity associated with it for someone to be sufficiently motivated to dispose of it. Until recently, nobody would acknowledge knowing what happened to it, or where it now is located, or if in fact it still exists. However, on April 7, 2012, it was reported that the former mayor of Mankato, Stan Christ, acknowledged that he surreptitiously "got rid of it." He was reported as having said that only three people (two of whom might now be dead, according to him) knew the answers to all the questions about its disappearance, but nobody was talking. And he said that he was sworn to secrecy.

In 2006 a history class at the Mankato State University took on the challenge of trying to find out what happened to the monument and locating it if possible. As the project was described in the Mankato Free Press on May 4, 2006, the investigators learned that the monument was last seen in the city storage yard in the mid 1990s. Nobody would acknowledge having seen it since, although obviously somebody knew what happened to it. Many rumors—that the monument was buried here or there or crushed up and buried under the new monument—were looked into, but none were substantiated. The student investigators met with the Mankato City Council. Before the meeting, the council had prepared a memo saying that the monument had been given to the Dakota, who took it away. Beyond that, the current city officials denied knowing anything more.

Then the students talked to some of the Dakota people, including Sheldon Wolfchild, who was tribal chairman at the Lower Sioux Reservation at the time. He denied any knowledge of the location of the monument, but he was quoted as having said, "In order to justify the war, they had to make us look savage."

The students also talked with Vernell Wabasha, one of the original promoters of the Mankato Powwow and wife of the hereditary chief of the Mdewakanton tribe. She was the only one who would admit knowing where the monument went.

"I know for sure where it's at," she was quoted as having said, and she called the monument "that derogatory rock." In the mid 1990s, besides having been very active with the Mankato Powwow since the very beginning, she was politically active and served on the State Indian Affairs Commission. Her opinion was highly respected and to the students investigating the disappearance of the monument she expressed the opinion that the monument should stay buried because it represented history that no one ought to be proud of. She wouldn't say anything more about it, adding only, "I keep telling you, it's a mystery. Our lips are sealed."

Unfortunately, whether or not that monument lies buried in some undisclosed location, as Vernell Wabasha implied, it is also buried in the memory of those who saw it or knew about it. Instead of being forgotten, as those who were responsible for its disappearance might have wished, it seems to have been resurrected by the mystery of how it vanished and where it went. And it also appears to be possible that we have not yet heard the last of it.

Notes

1. Churchill, 1.
2. Boutin.
3. Mankato Review, 1886.
4. Churchill, 180.
5. Churchill.
6. Churchill, 187.
7. Trenerry.
8. Lewis.
9. Lewis.
10. Hughes, 138.
11. Lewis.
12. Folwell.
13. Folwell, p. 289.

Chapter Two

Events That Led to the Powwow

THE FIRST LOCAL MODERN POWWOW took place in Mankato in 1972 and didn't just happen accidentally. It is something of a miracle that it happened at all. The events that led up to it occurred over a period of many years beginning in 1958 when Bud Lawrence, a Mankato businessman, first became a very close friend of Amos Owen, a spiritual leader, that by itself being a highly unlikely and improbable event, but apparently it was meant to be.

Bud Lawrence's wife, Shirley, was from Red Wing, Minnesota. Her parents still lived near there in the sixties, and Bud and Shirley would often travel from Mankato to visit them at their home near Red Wing. Bud heard about the good fishing south of Red Wing along the shore of the Mississippi River. He often ventured south from Red Wing to escape from the hubbub and pressures of the family gathering to do some relaxing fishing from the shore of the river. He found a good fishing hole near the railroad trestle where the Soo Line Railroad crossed the Vermilion River about half a mile from its confluence with the Mississippi. This was also, quite coincidentally, near the Prairie Island Indian Reservation.

On a hot summer day the area near the railroad trestle could be counted on to provide a peaceful place to fish in the shade and cooler temperatures under the trestle. It was a comfortable place to fish, and there were all kinds of fish under the trestle. The fish seemed to like the shade and the rush of the river currents around the structure of the trestle. Near the trestle one could catch crappies, sunfish, bass, northern pike, walleyes, and catfish. But those fishing had to know how to catch them. Obviously, one had to use the right bait for the different kinds of fish. Catfish, bottom feeders, liked worms, for example. Crappies and sunfish might go for worms too, but they liked little minnows even better, and they liked their meal suspended. Northern pike, walleyes, and bass liked bigger minnows or leeches or artificial lures cast from the riverbank.

On one particular Sunday morning, Bud had tried a variety of lures and bait near the trestle without much luck. He'd had a big fish on his line at one point, probably a northern, but it got off the hook before he could land it. He noticed a guy fishing on the downstream side of the trestle who seemed to be reeling in quite a few fish. Bud worked his way down there and saw that the man was catching crappies, one after another.

"Good morning," Bud said. "I see you're having good luck. I've been trying for a while but haven't caught anything."

The man glanced at Bud but said nothing.

After quite a long pause, Bud asked, "What are you using for bait?"

"Minnows," was the response.

Just then the man got another bite and pulled his rod back quickly, setting the hook. "Man, this feels like a good one."

Bud watched as the man skillfully reeled in his fish, not just horsing it in, but playing it a little and taking care to keep it from getting tangled in some brush in the water. The fish broke the surface of the water as it neared the shore.

"Get that net over there, will you? This is a really big one."

Bud rushed to grab the net lying on the ground nearby, and then rushed back to net the fish. He actually had to get into the water to do it, but he got the fish in the net on the first try. It really was a big one, about a two-pounder they estimated, quite large for a crappie.

As they started to get the fish off the hook and out of the net they saw that the hook had become tangled in the net and that the fish was not even on the hook at all.

"Thanks for your help," said the man after the fish was safely on his stringer. "I might have lost him if I'd had to get him in by myself. He must've been barely hooked."

"That's okay, I enjoyed it. That's a nice fish."

"That was good, the way you went into the water to get him. I likely would've lost him if I'd tried to pull him out much farther."

"Maybe so. Anyway, we got him."

They both smiled as they shook hands and exchanged names.

"I'm Bud Lawrence."

"And I'm Wally Wells."

Bud Lawrence looked somewhat like an American Indian, but Wally Wells actually was an American Indian. He was a Mdewakanton from the Prairie Island Reservation nearby.

"Are you enrolled here at Prairie Island?" Wally asked. "I don't think I ever saw you before."

"No," said Bud. "In fact, I'm not an Indian. I'm full-blooded German." (It is interesting to note that Bud is also part Norwegian, but he often called himself a full-blooded German.)

"You're kidding. You look like an Indian. You look more Indian than a lot of American Indians I know."

Bud was tall and slender, with coal-black, straight hair. He had a good tan from being out fishing so often, high cheek bones, and piercing dark-blue eyes (unless one looked closely, a person might not notice that his eyes were blue). He was a good looking fellow, a little like a "Hollywood Indian." Wally had similar features but was shorter and stockier than Bud, and he definitely was an Indian.

"Man, I wish I'd brought some minnows," Bud said. "You're having such good luck and the fish just don't seem to be biting on anything else today."

"Have some of mine," said Wally. "I've got plenty. I net 'em myself. There's a lot of 'em in a creek near here."

"Well, thank you. I'll take you up on that," said Bud.

"Just one thing," Wally said. "After you get your minnow on the hook and before you put it in the water, you need to spit on it. It's an old Indian trick. You catch more fish that way."

Bud laughed, but before he cast the minnow into the water he did spit on it. The two of them fished together for another hour, catching plenty of fish. Both Bud and Wally spit on the minnows, and the spit actually seemed to help. Between the two of them they had their legal limit of sixty nice big crappies after only an hour, and that was a lot of fish. They stopped at that point though they were having a good time—not only fishing but also getting acquainted with each other. In that short period of time they had become fast friends.

While fishing they had talked about many things. Wally told Bud about his membership in what was called the Indian Guide Program, a program for the sons and daughters (ages six to eight) of YMCA members, at the YMCA in Mankato. Bud expressed an interest in learning more about Indian ways so that he could contribute to the program. Wally suggested Bud meet his brother-in-law, Amos Owen, because Amos was widely known as a teacher of American Indian ways and traditions. Amos lived on the Prairie Island Reservation just a couple of miles from there, so when they left the river, they traveled together to Amos's home where they found him to be very receptive and welcoming to Bud, which was the beginning of yet another long and fast friendship.

It was certainly a red-letter day for Bud, who remained in close friendships with both Wally and Amos for the rest of their lives. Bud would visit them every time he and Shirley went to Red Wing to visit Shirley's parents. The routine became that Shirley would visit her parents while Bud went down to Prairie Island to visit with Walley and Amos, but mostly with Amos.

Amos was a tall, slender, good-looking man when Bud first met him. He had been born on August 4, 1916, on the Sisseton Indian Reservation in South Dakota, so when Bud met him in 1958 he was about forty-two years old, but he appeared older than his years. He had led a hard life. First he had grown up on a farm in South Dakota on a piece of property acquired through the Indian Reorganization Act. He then gave up farming when he moved with his mother to Prairie Island after his father died. His mother had grown up in the Prairie Island area, so when her husband died she went back there with her children.

Shortly after that, Amos was drafted into military service at the start of World War II. After five years in the army, and being in combat with the Japanese in the Philippines, he said that he couldn't farm anymore because, as he put it, he was "all shot up." At the end of the war he couldn't walk because of his wounds. He spent a considerable amount of time at a rehabilitation center in Walla Walla, Washington, where they told him at first that he likely would never be able to walk again. But after a year of rehab he was walking, though his physical impairment qualified him for a 100-percent veteran's disability pension. This was reduced in later years as he continued to overcome his disability.

Amos, like a lot of other American Indians, struggled with alcohol for a few years. For whatever the reason, culture shock, some vague genetic predisposition, or even something that nobody has yet thought of, many American Indians seem to be victimized by alcoholism as much as or more than just about any other ethnic group. Amos Owen was among them. But, in an odd way, his alcoholism may have led him to become the Dakota spiritual leader who was ultimately admired and respected throughout the Midwest.

Amos was a very intelligent man. His son Ray had estimated Amos's IQ to be in the neighborhood of 200. Ray said Amos had a photographic memory. He also said that when Amos achieved his sobriety and started down the "Red Road," he embraced American Indian spirituality whole-heartedly.

The fact that Amos won the struggle against alcoholism was a significant accomplishment by itself. He maintained his sobriety for the rest of his life and became a spiritual leader. He was, thereby, a model for many other American Indians who struggled with alcoholism. His sweat lodge Purification Ceremonies on Friday nights were something akin to an Alcoholics Anonymous meeting with many American Indians struggling with alcoholism in attendance. These visitors often came from distant places and stayed for extended visits to avail themselves of the good counsel and care that Amos gave to them.

In his youth Amos had attended an Indian school in Pipestone, Minnesota. There he was prohibited from speaking the Dakota language or practicing any Dakota traditions. He was punished if he engaged in those things, but he believed in the American Indian traditions and was a very spiritual man. He had his first spiritual vision at age twelve.

Even while he was attending the Indian school, he would often go to the stone quarry to watch the stone carving and pipe making that American Indians from all over the country were engaged in. So, when he started down the Red Road, according to Ray, he actually said, "I'm damned if I do [practice American Indian traditions] and damned if I don't, but I'm more damned if I don't." So he became the spiritual leader so many people came to know and respect.

Bud learned a great deal about the American Indians and their ways and traditions during his visits with Amos Owen. Amos was not only a spiritual leader among the Mdewakanton Dakota American Indians, but was broadly known for his leadership across the entire Midwest. He even became internationally known for his teachings, having lectured on American Indian spirituality in Europe.

Amos was also a maker of peace pipes. He would work on carving the pipes in a small building in the backyard of his home on the Prairie Island Reservation. That's where Bud spent many hours talking with him as he worked.

Over the course of many years, Amos presented Bud with three of the pipes he had made. The first was a broken one with no stem. Amos said that if Bud could get it fixed and make a stem for it, that pipe could represent their relationship. Bud had a brother-in-law who was a metalurgist who put the pipe back together with a special glue. For many years that pipe was the one smoked at the December 26th ceremonies.

The other two pipes, one small one of the kind that women often smoked and the other a buffalo pipe, remain in Bud's possession, but they are less meaningful to him than the broken one that was repaired. The repaired pipe is special. It represents the special relationship that Bud had with Amos and may also symbolically represent the repair of the broken relationship between the Dakota and the local white communities.

Amos was the chairman of the Prairie Island Tribal Community during the 1960s. He had held a sweat lodge ceremony in his backyard every Friday night and on other special occasions for many years, which he continued to do for the rest of his life. People of all kinds came to Prairie Island to consult Amos and to attend those sweats. Sometimes they traveled long distances to attend.

Despite his many accomplishments, Amos remained a very humble and unselfish man. Everyone who knew him liked him and, for some unknown reason, his closest friends called him "Polly." His Indian name was "Wiyohpeyata Hoksina" (Boy from the West).

One of the first things Bud learned about the local Dakota was that they were very poor. They often lacked even some of the essentials for a healthy life and were often hungry. The rate of employment in the Prairie Island community was very low and even those with jobs had incomes well below the average for most communities. Bud responded to this by persuading the Methodist Church in Kasson, Minnesota, to launch a clothing drive for the Dakota at Prairie Island. Soon after, truckloads of clothing began arriving.

Bud had grown up in Kasson and had graduated from high school there in 1949 and was still well acquainted with the community. He had played basketball and football during his school years. Even then he had looked Indian, and he recalled overhearing the opponent's coach at a basketball game telling his boys, "Cover that Indian better," when Bud was having an exceptional night of good shooting.

Getting Amos to go to Mankato to give talks to the schools and Indian Guide group at the YMCA was easy. It seemed to be Amos's calling to talk about Dakota ways and traditions, and he was always more than willing to do it. Amos also managed to persuade several other Dakota to join him in these talks. Vernell and Ernie Wabasha were regulars. The idea was to replace the misinformation being given to the kids in schools with accurate information less critical of American Indians. Instead of the American Indians being depicted as inhumane savages, they clearly demonstrated that American Indians were sensitive human beings but simply with a different culture.

Then, to reciprocate and honor Amos Owen's election as tribal chairmen at Prairie Island, and to gain recognition for the Indian Guide Program at the YMCA in Mankato, Bud and his friend Barry Blackhawk, a Winnebago (Hochunk) Indian and a student at Mankato State College, organized a run from Mankato to Prairie Island in 1965. They trained for the trip to Prairie Island by running about ten miles a day to get in shape.

The day they actually started out for Prairie Island, they began the trip in the midst of a thunderstorm and made a large part of the run in ninety-five degree heat. It was so hot that when they reached Cannon Lake, a long stretch of water that paralleled their route, they took the time to enter the lake up to their necks in water to refresh themselves and get some relief from the heat.

Nevertheless, they completed the run to Prairie Island in less than two days, running and walking for a total of twenty-seven and a half hours and camping out one night near Northfield. It turned out to be a successful promotion resulting in some newspaper articles.

Bob Rolfes, another Indian Guide Program participant, accompanied them in a car "riding shotgun," as Bud called it, backing them up with needed support such as providing drinking water and snacks along the way and grilled steaks in their camp near Northfield at the end of the first exhausting day.

In the car with Bob were his son (Bobby), Bud's son (Alan), and Barry's son (Brad). The boys were all members of the YMCA's Indian Guide program. Going from Mankato to near Northfield on foot in extreme weather in one day was a physical accomplishment that would be impossible for most people. And then to continue on the next day to Prairie Island must certainly have been torturous.

And in fact it was tortuous. Both Bud and Barry developed such severe blisters on their feet that the last leg of the run was very difficult. At one point, Barry was resigned to giving up because of the pain that he was experiencing. He had a blister on one of his little toes that was causing some displacement of the toenail. Every step that he took was pure agony.

He stopped to examine his toe and told Bud, "You'll have to go on without me because I just can't do it."

Bud was reluctant to go on without Barry, but when he saw Barry's toe he did agree to do so and went down the road alone. Soon after going over the next hill, however, he looked back and saw Barry coming up behind him and closing fast.

When Barry caught up he said, "I pulled the toenail off and the pain went away."

As Bud and Barry ran down a country road with the town behind them out of sight and the town ahead not in view, they passed a herd of about twenty Holstein heifers not far from the fence just on the other side of the ditch. The cows interrupted their grazing to stare at the passing runners. In unison, the gaze of the whole herd of Holstein cows followed them as they passed on the road. Just in case Bud hadn't noticed what was happening, Barry pointed it out.

"Hey, Bud. Look at those cows. See how they're following us with their eyes?"

"Yeah, I saw that."

"Well, it reminded me of something. That's the way the white clerks look at me when I go into a store sometimes. Even in a grocery store."

"Well, maybe they never saw anyone that looked quite like you before. I bet these cows never saw anyone running down this road before. Lots of cars, but not people running."

"That's what I mean. They don't see a lot of American Indians in Mankato."

When they neared the Prairie Island Reservation at the end of the run, they saw a group of American Indians on horseback had come out to greet them. They turned out to be most of the tribal council at the Prairie Island Reservation, including Amos Owen who was chairman of the council at the time. The others were Chris Leith, Ed Jefferson, and Wally Wells, who were all members of the council.

Bud and Barry raced toward the group to see who could get there first, but they arrived with a tie. Then they all traveled together the remaining short distance into the arena of a small Powwow that was already under way. The emcee was from the Turtle Mountain Chippewa Reservation. He introduced them to the crowd and told them about their run. With tongue in cheek, he introduced Barry Blackhawk as a "Mankato State College Winnebago."

Then he asked Bud, "Where are you enrolled?"

Bud replied, "Nowhere. I'm a German-Norwegian."

The Emcee was a little puzzled by this response because Bud looked as much like an Indian as anyone.

"Come on. This is no time to fool around."

"No fooling," said Bud. "I'm not an Indian."

The emcee then introduced Bud, facetiously, as a "German Chippewa." This had to be a teasing appellation because the Dakota were not especially fond of the German immigrants because of the way they had been treated by them, and in the past the Dakota had been at war with the Chippewa (Ojibwe) American Indians for many generations.

Later that same year a mini-Powwow was held in the gymnasium at the Mankato YMCA with Amos Owen leading the activities with Wally Wells, Ed Jefferson, and Chris Leith in attendance and adding their knowledge and expertise to the ceremonies. They all had their families there with them. Approximately 100 kids in the Indian Guide Program attended the Powwow along with their parents. A highlight of this mini-powwow was the presentation to the YMCA of a plaque made of birch bark commemorating the support of the YMCA for its educational programs regarding the American Indians. The plaque also honored Bud Lawrence and Barry Blackhawk for their run to Prairie Island.

Several years after that, in 1969, Bud Lawrence went on foot again from Mankato to Prairie Island, this time with Jim Buckley accompanying him, after Bud talked him into it. Jim Buckley was a city boy in his youth, graduating from Columbia Heights High School in Minneapolis. He had completed college at the University of Minnesota in 1951. At the age of thirty he was the director of the Mankato YMCA.

Jim described the walk as one requiring great endurance, which was not surprising coming from a man who was essentially a white collar worker who was not used to much physical exertion, although he exercised regularly. He was slight of build, not as tall as Bud, and his stride was shorter than Bud's.

At one point during the walk, Jim sat down completely out of breath and totally spent and said, according to Bud, "Bud Lawrence, are you trying to kill me?" But after a short rest they continued on their way.

When I talked to Jim about the walk, he acknowledged that the walk was a difficult one, but said, as if to save face, "At the end it was Bud who had blisters on his feet, not me."

They had started out at 4:00 a.m. and covered a lot of ground before the heat began to get to them, and then the temperature shot up and the day became a hot one. A third walker accompanied them for awhile. This was Merrill Claridge, an older man in his sixties at the time, who walked with Jim and Bud as far as Madison Lake, about ten miles east of Mankato, where he gave up. Despite his age, he was able to keep up with the much younger guys that far, but from the beginning he had no intention of completing the whole walk.

When Bud and Jim reached Morristown they lunched briefly on a chocolate milk shake for relief from the heat and then were on their way again. There was not much preparation or planning for the walk and Bud and Jim more or less "winged it" all the way. They had no idea where or how they would spend the night along the way, but when darkness was falling they had put about forty miles behind them and they walked up to a motel near Cannon Falls. They found that it was closed, no longer in business and soon to be razed to make room for a new road. However, the people who lived there gave them a complementary room, having heard about them and their walk on the radio.

The motivation for the walk was once again to honor Amos Owen for all of his efforts to educate people everywhere about Indian history and it's traditions, and to promote the Indian Guide Program at the Mankato YMCA as well.

When they arrived at Prairie Island late in the afternoon of the second day, there was again a small powwow under way, but this time they were greeted with a little less fanfare. They simply walked into the arena where they were recognized and that was about it. Although Wally's wife, Gertrude ("Pudge") Wells, made a joke about how nice it would have been to have Jim Buckley's red hair on her teepee pole.

One more walk to Prairie Island for the purpose of honoring Amos Owen should be mentioned. Carie Robb, Marilyn Hardt, and three other women walked from Mankato to Prairie Island for just that purpose. It took three days to complete the trip. Amos Owen had a great number of devotees who admired and appreciated his work and accomplishments.

Chapter Three

The First Reconciliation Powwow

I N 1972 THE VERY FIRST "RECONCILIATION POWWOW" took place in Mankato.
The word "powwow" comes from an Algonquian expression, "pau wau,"
which means, "He dreams" or conjuror. By extension, it also means "medicine
man" or spiritual leader."

"Powwow" is defined in *Webster's New Twentieth Century Dictionary of the English Language*[1] as:

1. Among North American Indians, a priest or Medicine Man.
2. Among North American Indians, a ceremony to conjure the cure of disease, success in war, etc., usually accompanied by magic, feasting, and noise.
3. A conference of or with North American Indians.

After attending powwows for more than twenty years I have never heard the word "powwow" used in accordance with the first two definitions, but the third definition comes close to the way the word is used at the Mankato Powwow, although the definition is much too meager. The Mankato Powwow is much more than merely a conference. To the American Indians, a powwow is thought to be a living thing with a spirit of its own that brings people together to celebrate whatever needs celebrating, to sing and dance and engage in many different cultural activities from many different cultures.

The Mankato Powwow is sometimes called a "*wacipi*" (pronounced wah-chee-pee). This is the Dakota word for "dance." "Powwow" and "*wacipi*" are sometimes used almost synonymously, but "powwow" is the word with broadest meaning. A powwow can and usually does have a *wacipi* within it, but a powwow is much more than a dance. What a powwow actually is will be elaborated in some detail in the course of this book.

With all of the powwow experiences that Bud and Amos and Jim had behind them, it is not surprising that the notion of having a big powwow in Mankato would somehow emerge in their thinking. Amos had talked about this possibility many times, but it is something of a surprise that the idea first seemed to crystallize for Bud and Jim while they were out jogging as a routine part of their exercise. They thought that a big powwow could possibly be a good fund raiser for youth programs at the YMCA. The money would be very helpful for new equipment at the YMCA, free memberships to the YMCA for boys and girls who needed financial help, or for scholarships to the YMCA summer programs at Camp Patterson on Lake Washington.

At the first opportunity, they talked with Amos Owen about their idea. Amos had a different, broader perspective. To Amos, a powwow in Mankato might be a way of bringing the Dakota back to an area that had once very important to them, and it might also be a way of healing the fractured relationships between the local white communities and the Dakota people. Consequently, Amos not only agreed to the idea, but he was also very enthusiastic and optimistic about it and in favor of going ahead with it as soon as possible. They would try to get the YMCA to sponsor it.

Jim Buckley was a bit hesitant. He was the director of the YMCA at the time, but he didn't own the place and couldn't say with any kind of certainty how the organization would respond to the idea of sponsoring a powwow despite the fact that the Indian Guide Program was quite successful and popular. It took some persuasion from Bud and Jim to get the go ahead for it, but in the end the YMCA did agree to it and the Y's Mens Club ultimately became the main work force at the 1972 Powwow.

Amos Owen, Bud Lawrence, and Jim Buckley started right away to plan for the powwow. Amos was to contact people in the Indian communities and get their support for it. Bud and Jim would talk with the "Y's Men's" Club at the YMCA to see if they could get some financial support and some volunteer help for a powwow in Mankato. The three of them found enthusiastic support from both sides, and before long plans and preparations for the powwow were well under way.

A great deal of preparation went into getting that first powwow to take place. The American Indians that Amos recruited to help plan the powwow were a very special group who, at their own expense, drove to Mankato from long distances to participate in many planning meetings held in Jim Buckley's office at the YMCA. Many such meetings took place throughout the spring and summer of 1972. By September, the planning was complete and it was time to put the plans into action.

Amos sent notices to all the American Indian communities in a wide area that the powwow would be held at the Key City Ballpark (also called the Franklin Rogers Ballpark) in Mankato. Amos also attended all the powwows held in the

Midwest area and distributed flyers about the new Mankato Powwow to whomever would display them. It would happen the third weekend in September. The timing of it was to coincide with the nearby Farm Fest activities in Owatonna which was known to attract people from all over the world. The idea was that visitors at the Farm Fest might also like to see a powwow and a good attendance at the powwow would be guaranteed. To add to the publicity for the Mankato Powwow, Bud and Jim talked about it on the local radio and television stations and gave information about it to the local newspapers.

Meals would be provided for dance participants. Dancers would also be allowed to camp at the ballpark, which would serve as powwow grounds. Reimbursement for mileage expenses would be provided to those from out of state (up to 300 miles). The Y's Men Club at the YMCA agreed to help out as volunteers at the powwow and to back up the powwow with funding. The decision to have the powwow coincide with Farm Fest backfired, however, and the powwow ended up almost $1,200 in the hole, which the Y's Men Club made good on. The powwow just couldn't compete with the likes of Bob Hope at the Farm Fest. Fewer spectators than expected visited the powwow. The $1,200 loss at the powwow was a lot of money in those days. Nevertheless, despite the financial loss to the Y's Men Club, the powwow was considered to have been a success because a large number of people did attend it, after all, and because for the first time in 110 years the Dakota appeared to be welcome in the area.

The first powwow was a comparatively simple affair, starting with the relatively small number of notices that Amos Owen sent out to American Indian communities and various individuals, letting them know about the event and asking them to come and dance. This first powwow was a dance contest powwow. Over $1,200 in prizes were to be awarded to the winners of contests in several dance categories. No special ceremonies were planned to be held, except for one—that ceremony was a prayer by Amos Owen to put an end to the hostilities that had continued since the war between the whites and the American Indians in the Mankato-New Ulm area.

While preparations for the powwow were still being made, there was a lot of concern over whether anybody would actually attend it. After all, there was still some evidence that the local white community remained antagonistic to the American Indians, and few American Indians ventured to pass through the area in the daytime. Those circumstances were part of the motivation for this reconciliation powwow. The powwow was to be a catalyst for bringing American Indians back to the area and for getting the local white population to have a better attitude about them. Nobody (except the vandals themselves, of course) knew whether it was American Indians or whites throwing red paint on the monument marking the place where the thirty-eight warriors were hanged in 1862, but it was the hope of all who were involved with the powwow that the anger underlying such vandalism would be eliminated. Tensions were high in the days just before the powwow.

Bud Lawrence approached Amos Owen one day shortly before the powwow to ask, "What if we go to all this trouble to have this big powwow and nobody shows up for it?"

Amos replied, "Don't worry. Tomorrow morning the Dakota will come."

On Friday evening there were still few people at the powwow and the concerns that the powwow would fail to attract many people grew stronger. There were no drums at the powwow at all on the first evening, only recorded music of drumming. The only dancer there on Friday night was Harvey Davenport, a Mesquakie Indian from Iowa, who was also one of the vendors. Nevertheless, he did dance, all by himself, to get the powwow started. But eventually, Amos Owen was proven to be right when many people did come. By Saturday evening the whole outfield of the ballpark was filled with campers, mostly dancers and vendors. And in addition there were about one hundred spectators who passed through the gate to visit the powwow. Even with that small number, Vernell Wabasha later complained that she was so busy at the gate that she had little time to spend at the powwow. She had only one helper, Sally Beaulieu.

There were only a few concessions, perhaps five, and one of those was from the Mankato Chamber of Commerce, the "Mrs. Jaycee's," who sold hamburgers and gave the profits from this concession to the powwow. For most of the remainder of the weekend, two drum groups provided drumming and singing and there were many more dancers. Everyone agreed that the powwow was a huge success with both American Indians and whites attending in reasonably good numbers. As successful as it was, however, it was going to take more than one powwow to completely end the enmity that had existed between the American Indians and the local white communities for at least 110 years.

The following year, in 1973, there was no powwow. There were likely multiple reasons for this, but one big one was the fact that the Y's Men Club could not afford it nor was it willing to foot the bill again. Also, it was possible that nobody had even conceived of the powwow as being an annual event. The first powwow might have been thought of as a one-time affair. But when September 1973 rolled around and there was no powwow in the offing, a lot of people, especially the American Indians and the Mankato Chamber of Commerce, began to wonder, "Why not?" And then the ball started rolling again—planning meetings started taking place for the powwow to be held in 1974. All the same people were involved. This time there was more confidence and fewer questions and problems to be worked out. What worked well before, in 1972, would likely work well again. Fewer meetings were necessary. The planning group or committee had learned a great deal from their experience in 1972.

There was a considerable bump in the road to the 1974 Powwow when the Mankato Chamber of Commerce could no longer offer financial assistance. The powwow committee of the time, largely the original people who got the powwow going in the first place, decided to hold a fund-raising dance. The $500 raised by that dance was the seed money needed for the next powwow. With this small starting pot they managed to have a successful powwow in 1974.

The 1974 Powwow still had no financial backing, but the Chamber of Commerce and the Zonta Club in Mankato were co-sponsors of it and provided a small (but important) amount of financial support. This may have been the first public service offered by the Zonta Club, which was only newly chartered in Mankato. Carie Robb was a charter member of the Zonta Club and led the way to soliciting support for the powwow in 1974.

Carie Robb and her husband, Donovan, were instrumental in generating the financial stake for the 1974 Powwow by promoting the dance held at the Kato Ballroom in Mankato to benefit the powwow. The use of the ballroom was provided free of charge by the owner of the ballroom, Joe Martinka, who was a friend of Carie. The $500 in proceeds obtained from the dance was the first seed money that actually got the powwow going again.

To put the powwow on firmer ground the planners took the bull by the horns and began soliciting the local community and local businesses for support. By September 1974 the second powwow in Mankato was ready to be held. The local community and local businesses were supportive because they agreed with the purposes of the powwow and because it was a major event in Mankato that brought a lot of business into town. Many donations came, including the use of space to conduct the event, food for meals at the powwow, the use of a bandstand, electricity for lights, and the lights themselves. Even without being asked, the City of Mankato offered the use of Sibley Park free of charge. The local community seemed to be welcoming not only the American Indians, but the powwow as well. That was additional evidence that the powwow in 1972 had been a success.

In every year since 1974 when it was held at Sibley Park, the powwow has taken place as an annual event. Succeeding powwows have had similar success and were able to grow. Better efforts were made to advertise the powwow, and many more spectators showed up for it. Bud Lawrence has said, "A good gate guarantees a good powwow." Bud and Jim Buckley were often seen working at the gate themselves, selling buttons, soliciting visitors for donations to help the dancers. The powwow continued at Sibley Park through 1979.

All of the Indian communities, even some distant ones, became more supportive of the powwow when they were more able to provide financial support after the advent of Indian casinos. After a few years the powwow officials were able to compensate such people as the spiritual leader, the emcees, and the arena director, not with a lot of money but with a stipend that would at least cover their expenses.

For several years Amos Owen would not accept any expense money though he was not wealthy and he traveled quite a distance from Prairie Island to Mankato for the powwow. He covered his own expenses and was there every year until his death in 1990. But one year he did accept $250.00. He took the cash handed to him and quickly disappeared. Soon after, he returned with a big grin saying that he felt "real good." When asked what that was all about, he said he had given the money away to people who really needed it. He had walked among the campers and dancers and gave money to some who needed gas money to get home. His wife, Ione, scolded him for this because they didn't have money for their own needs.

Bill Bassett, city manager of Mankato, and Amos Owen became quite good friends. They didn't pal together like Bud and Amos did, but whenever they did cross paths doing business about the Mankato Powwow, they seemed to get along with each other especially well. In fact, they got along so well that Amos gave Bill a pipe that he had carved.

On one occasion while Amos was close to the end of his life, Bud was preparing to visit Amos in the hospital. He stopped by Bill Bassett's office and informed Bill that Amos's daughter, Linda, had called and said that Amos was likely to pass on. He asked Bill if he would like to go see Amos before he died. Bill's desk was piled high with work and he regretfully declined to go with Bud. Bud made the trip by himself, and Amos lived a while longer after that. The next time Linda called, she was quite sure that Amos was very close to passing away and Bud went again to see him.

When he entered Amos's hospital room, Amos greeted him excitedly, saying, "Guess who came to see me! Bill Bassett! He came all the way down here to see me!"

Well, Amos had ministered and lectured to a lot of important people, but for some reason Bill Bassett was special to him. Perhaps it was because Bill was an important help in the fulfillment of Amos's vision for Mankato, the reconciliation of the American Indian and white communities. In any case, he seemed to have been as pleased with Bassett's visit as he might have been with a visit from the president of the United States.

The next time Bud went to visit Amos was the last time before Amos did pass away. Amos had been allowed to go home to die. As Bud entered a room in the house where Amos was sitting, Amos started to get up to greet him, but Bud insisted he should stay where he was. Amos was obviously very weak and couldn't even talk. Bud did all the talking, but Amos listened and seemed to have an appreciation for Bud's reminiscences about the old days and many of the things that they had experienced together. That was the last time Bud saw Amos alive. Amos died the next day, June 4, 1990, at his home on the Prairie Island Reservation after a two-year battle with cancer.

His passing was a great loss to the powwow, and to the Prairie Island community that he had served for so long, as well as to the multitude of people to whom he gave spiritual guidance. His funeral was like one for a head of state. One local newspaper, *The Red Wing Republican*, on June 9, 1990, reported that he was taken to his grave over a four-mile route in a flag-covered coffin on a horse-drawn bier followed by a road full of mourners, more than 300. He was buried next to his mother according to his own wish, "among the cottonwood trees and near the river." (See color plate of Amos Owen.)

* * *

DURING THE FIRST POWWOW IN 1972 many of those who attended insist that a flock of thirty-eight bald eagles circled overhead while Amos and a few others prayed for reconciliation of the Indian and white communities. The number of eagles matched exactly the number of Dakota warriors hanged in 1862 and who were being honored at the powwow. Those who saw them believed that the eagles were the spirits of the hanged warriors. Amos Owen, the spiritual leader of that first powwow, saw them and called them to the attention of some of the other people nearby. These included Norman Crooks and Jim Buckley. All who were present saw at least some of the thirty-eight eagles. Amos told them the eagles were the spirits of the thirty-eight warriors.

I heard this story since becoming involved with the powwow, but I remained skeptical that there were that many eagles even in the whole state of Minnesota, let alone circling in a flock over this first powwow. Eagles had become rare in Minnesota, but at that time, in 1972, they were making a big comeback in numbers because of the ban of DDT, a weed killer which had been secondarily poisoning a lot of wildlife. In predatory birds, like eagles and perigrin falcons, ingestion of DDT in their food chains caused thin-shelled eggs that didn't survive incubation. But after the ban of DDT, predatory birds began to recover. Nevertheless, I could not believe that anyone would have seen thirty-eight eagles in a flock like that. Since then I've changed my opinion about that story. I now believe these were actually the spirits of the thirty-eight hanged warriors in the form of eagles, just as those who saw them claimed.

* * *

SUMMER IS THE SEASON FOR POWWOWS and many are held in various places. Powwow vendors go from one to another, traveling what is called the powwow "circuit," and many of the dancers do that too. The Mankato Powwow, held the third week in September each year, is the last local outdoor powwow of the season. Later powwows take place indoors or in the southern part of the Untied States.

The Mankato Powwow continued to be held in Sibley Park every year during the third weekend in September from 1974 through 1978. Then the City of Mankato suggested that it should have a permanent location at a place near Sibley Park but across the Blue Earth River. That place was given the name "Wokiksuye Makoce" (Land of Memories) by Amos Owen. He gave it that name because it is the place where the American Indians had powwows before the white man came to the area. Since 1979 that is where the modern reconciliation powwows have been held. It is a place which the American Indians revere as having a very high level of spiritual significance.

Chapter Four

Getting Organized

T HE FIRST POWWOW IN 1972 had no Mdewakanton Club or association and no formal organization at all. The organizers of the powwow more or less just flew by the seat of their pants to get it off the ground. Aside from the founders, Amos Owen, Bud Lawrence, and Jim Buckley, who had the inspiration for the powwow to begin with, the organizers were mainly the group of close friends Amos Owen rounded up to help get things going. Who better to get a powwow going than a group of American Indians? They were Wally and Gertrude Wells; Ernie Wabasha, the hereditary chief of the Mdewakanton, and his wife Vernell; Norman and Edith Crooks; and Amos and Rose Crooks; and Big Dave Larsen. In 2005 a memorial plaque was established at Land of Memories Park to commemorate their contribution to getting the powwow established in Mankato, and the road through the park was named Amos Owen Lane.

The sign at the entrance to the park. (Author's personal collection)

The sign on Amos Owen Lane in Land of Memories Park. (Author's personal collection)

The organizers all had previous experience with putting a powwow together, of course, but this powwow was new to them in some ways because it was the first one that they had organized that was not held on an American Indian reservation. Held in the middle of a white community, some new and different rules applied. Some consideration had to be given to meeting the standards of the local health department, for example. What were the requirements for cleanliness in the food concessions? Was it necessary for the food vendors to be licensed? What kind of toileting facilities would be necessary for the vendors, campers, and spectators? What provisions were needed for emergencies? None of these matters were likely to pose issues at a powwow on a reservation, but what about in the City of Mankato? Would the organizers be arrested as law breakers for non-compliance with some or any of the community's rules? All of these matters were negotiated and worked out with the authorities of the City of Mankato before the event took place. Nevertheless, throughout the 1970s the Mdewakanton Club had no insurance, and food vendors were not required to have a Department of Health permit. Amos Owen's position on these matters was, "American Indians do not sue one another." Luckily, nobody got hurt, there were no serious accidents, and nobody got sick from the food.

Preparations for that first powwow in 1972 were made by the founders and some volunteers from the YMCA. That powwow was smaller than all of those to follow, but it was still a lot of work to put even a small powwow together. When it developed that the powwow would become an annual affair, it became apparent that some kind of organization was needed and consequently the Mdewakanton Club was created.

The Mdewakanton Club has membership comprised mostly of citizens of the local white communities, but it started out with more American Indians in it than whites because the initial members included all those American Indians who helped create the first Reconciliation Powwow in 1972. Some of these have remained very actively involved with the club ever since then, but after all the intervening years, many of those original people are now deceased. In recent years the membership has been mostly comprised of people who live in or near Mankato where the meetings of the club are held, and most of these people are white. As has been stated, the American Indians were exiled from the area long ago. Some American Indians who might like to attend the meetings would have to travel a considerable distance to get there. Occasionally, some did come from far away. In recent years, more of them are once again coming and participating.

The membership changes frequently as people come and go, but there are usually about thirty to forty active members with about half of them attending what often have been monthly meetings. All kinds of people join the membership. Quite a few have been from the faculty of Mankato State University. All the members seem to have personal reasons for participating. Sometimes they have their own agenda for what they want to accomplish through their membership; these don't last long. If they finish what they set out to do, or if they encounter conflict with the general goals of the club or association, or if too much is asked of them, they leave quickly. But some members have been with the association from the very beginning. Most members just want to support the general mission of the Association.

Because it evolved that most of the members have been non-American Indians, the need for the "Dakota Advisory Committee" developed. This committee, comprised of representatives of the Dakota Indian communities, is made up of American Indians who will help to keep the activities of the association culturally correct. Even though many individuals in the Mdewakanton Association are relatively well informed about American Indian ways and traditions, it happens sometimes that important questions arise for which nobody in the group has an answer. The advisory committee serves as a consultant at those times. In addition, they have responsibilities regarding the powwow, like setting its theme, choosing the host drum and the arena director and emcees. The involvement of the advisory committee is essential to keep the powwow absolutely authentic.

The mission of the Mdewakanton Club, as stated in the Articles of Incorporation and the adopted Bylaws, is to "create a climate for positive interactions and relationships between people, with an emphasis on American Indians and non-American Indians. We foster these interactions and relationships through learning, teaching and promoting understanding of the American Indian history, culture, and lifestyles with a special emphasis on the Mdewakanton Dakota." When it was incorporated as a private non-profit organization the club's name was changed from "Mdewakanton Club" to "Mahkato Mdewakanton Association".

The work of sponsoring (and preparing for) a powwow amounts to a highly challenging list of things to do, many of which must be done ahead of the arrival of the campers, dancers, and spectators. Just a cursory review of the tasks laid out by the Mdewakanton Association for a fairly recent powwow gives an idea of how much work is involved and why the organization, the Mdewakanton Association, was necessary. Despite the loftiness of the mission statement, getting two cultures to come together, most of the work of the association boils down to the nitty-gritty labor of laying the groundwork for the annual powwow, which is now a traditional rather than a competition powwow.

Letters of solicitation are sent (and/or visits made) to many supporters of the powwow months before it takes place. Requests for financial support are sent to the usual major donors, the tribal offices of the American Indian communities in Minnesota. Support is also requested from members of the Mankato and North Mankato Chambers of Commerce. Other sources of financial support are also explored. The bandstand used by the emcees at the powwow is borrowed from the City of North Mankato, and it must be reserved early or it might not be available when needed. Contact must be made with various sources of volunteers, such as the sheriff's Sentence-to-Serve Program (to mention just one of them), to ensure that the help needed for the powwow will be available. Some of these sources are contacted repeatedly to guarantee that this important help is obtained.

The banners and crowns for the winners of the Miss Mahkato and Junior Miss Mahkato contests must be ordered in time for them to be custom made and completed before the contests are held.

Some of the arrangements for the powwow are routine repetitions of the arrangements made in previous years and need only to be re-established. For example, the use of the park must be reserved for the days when the powwow will be held, making sure that the Park Department's personnel are informed of the many tasks we need them to do, such as when we need flood lights for the arena installed, getting the grass in the powwow area mowed, and many other smaller tasks they accomplish. They are there the whole weekend to monitor the use of the park and help trouble-shoot anything that goes wrong.

The powwow attracts thousands of spectators who enjoy food and snacks and drinks sold on paper plates and in paper cups, thereby generating mountains of trash. The Grounds Committee of the Mdewakanton Association takes care of all this trash. The park has many trash receptacles scattered throughout the camping area, but the grounds crew puts out about fifty extra trash barrels. So much trash is produced that all of them must be emptied at least once during the weekend.

The grounds crew learned the hard way to empty the barrels late on Saturday. Nobody was bothering to empty them, and they were all more than full, especially the ones near food concessions. In fact, so much trash was piled on and around some of them that the barrels disappeared in the middle of the pile. Paul Covey was on the grounds crew at the time and solved the trash emergency by compacting the trash in the barrel. The way he did this was to lift his five-year-old boy to the top of the trash pile and have him dance on it in the barrel. The boy seemed to enjoy doing what could be called the "Garbage Stomp," a dance step a lot like what one might do when mashing grapes. This crushed the paper cups and plates together and reduced the volume of trash significantly. With that done (a couple of times at each barrel as they picked up the trash on the ground), they moved on to the next overflowing barrel and started all over. Soon, the immediate emergency was resolved, at least temporarily. Eventually, the barrels were emptied into three large dumpsters and one smaller one provided by the association and removed after the park was cleaned up of all litter on Monday morning. Each large dumpster was capable of containing thirty cubic yards of compacted trash, and the smaller one ten cubic yards. By the time these dumpsters were hauled off by the sanitation company, they were all full and piled high.

The large number of spectators would overwhelm the toilet facilities normally available at the park, so the Mdewakanton Association rents about thirty porta-potties and has them delivered and placed strategically throughout the pow-wow area.

As the time for the Powwow nears, the members of the Mdewakanton Association are all busy with one thing or another. Firewood for the Spirit Fire at the sweat lodge is ordered and more wood for the campers is obtained and distributed to campsites. Planks for benches around the circle are trucked in, along with cement blocks to put them on. The wooden benches are for the dancers with bustles. The benches enable them to sit down without damaging their regalia. Fourteen bleachers are moved into place for the spectators to view the dancing. The flag poles in the middle of the arena always need some maintenance. The club's storage shed is emptied and its contents are trucked to the powwow area. Its contents include pots and pans for the cook shack, flags for the arena, electrical extension cords, tools, and anything else with utility left over from previous years, such as many signs and hardware for barriers and fences to be used for traffic and crowd control. The camp kitchen or "cook shack" must be cleaned and made operational and a refrigerator trailer obtained for it. Habitation quarters (a trailer borrowed from a local RV dealer) for the emergency first aid and security people must be obtained, delivered to the park, and put into place. The picnic tables scattered throughout the park are moved to the area where Education Day activities will take place on Friday. They are placed in a large circle and each will serve as a learning station.

Also as the time for the powwow approaches, decisions have to be made regarding who will be the emcees at the powwow, who will be the arena director, and who will serve as the host drum. All of these are paid a stipend and an informal contract must be established with them. They are provided accommodations in a local motel for at least two nights and rooms must be reserved. Although the Dakota Advisory Committee makes these decisions, the Mdewakanton Association must approve all of these expenses. The Advisory Committee also decides what special focus the powwow will have, if any, and what ceremonies will be scheduled in the powwow program. A sound system must be installed in the bandstand for use by the emcees and the host drum.

When the vendors begin to arrive they must be given assigned spots in the outer circle. Before that happens, the lots for the vendors must be marked on the ground so they will know what space and how much space they have in which to set up. The Mdewakanton Association assigns one member the responsibility of negotiating with the vendors, taking care of them, collecting the space rental money from them, and keeping them in line with the rules set down for the powwow. This person is the vendor coordinator. This often turns out to be a very difficult job. The coordinator monitors the vendors' wares and tries to enforce the rule that all merchandise should be authentically American Indian in its origin. Chinese made knockoffs of American Indian crafted items, for example, are not allowed. And certain items like explosive things, fireworks and firecrackers, are not allowed. Merchandise that is any kind of weaponry, like ninja throwing stars, whips, or knives that could hurt someone, are not allowed. If a vendor is found hawking any of these things, he or she is asked to put them away and not sell them. If they won't or don't comply they are required to leave.

Any merchandise that is a spiritually sacred object is also prohibited from being sold by the vendors. Painted buffalo skulls, blessed peace pipes, and anything with genuine eagle feathers are examples of such merchandise. The vendors often get big money for such things and they are highly motivated to hawk them. One woman who was required to leave the powwow for selling painted buffalo skulls simply set up her shop on the side of the street leading to the powwow. When she was asked to stop selling there, she protested, saying that it was her legal right to do what she was doing. Law enforcement officials and governmental officials from the City of Mankato and from Blue Earth County were called by powwow officials. When they showed up, they hesitated before doing anything because some argued they might be violating her legal or human rights if they were to close her down. Before they could do anything to stop her, she sold all her buffalo skulls and packed up her gear and departed from the area leaving all those officials still arguing about whether they could legally stop her.

One of the biggest problems in dealing with the vendors is the tendency they have to want to use too much electricity. They are informed in advance that electricity is available for lights only. If they need more power than that, it must come from their own generator. Electricity is supplied free of charge by the City of Mankato, which is, by itself, a very generous donation by the local community and its citizens. At many powwows no electricity is available to the vendors. One vendor said that at another powwow he had to string wire for over 500 feet to obtain electricity. Though the Mankato Powwow makes electricity for lights convenient to them, some of the vendors want to plug in their cooking appliances and their RVs, heaters, refrigerators, and air conditioners, and when they do that they blow circuit breakers, and the lights go out for several vendors around them. This makes a lot of them mad and it spoils the fun for everyone involved. Also, it sometimes knocks out the sound system and puts a temporary halt to the dancing and activities in the arena. So the "lights only rule" must be strictly enforced.

Every year, all the volunteers must be registered and assigned all of the numerous tasks they help to accomplish. They help with the flow of traffic, parking, picking up litter, assisting in the kitchen and getting food to elders, as well as various other kinds of errands. Most of the volunteers are young people from schools, nearby colleges, churches, or organizations like the YMCA or Boy Scouts and Girl Scouts. The Sheriff's Department brings the sentenced-to-serve offenders out to the powwow several times during and after the powwow to (ironically) "police" the grounds, helping with the cleanup of the park. Equally ironic was the time I allowed them to use my four-wheel-drive Ranger pickup to help with the job of Monday morning cleanup. At that time, the starter switch on the truck was malfunctioning. To start the truck it was necessary to go under the hood and, with a screwdriver, short out the wires to the poles of the starter to get it going. They laughed as I instructed them on how to do this. I then realized I was teaching a bunch of young law breakers how to hot wire a car.

* * *

THE DANCERS MUST BE REGISTERED. They are given a number that is attached to their regalia, and their participation in the Grand Entry is monitored to give them credit for the dancing they actually did. To help them with their travel expenses, they are given a share of the monies received from donations, gate receipts, and rentals to vendors. By the end of the powwow weekend, the Mdewakanton Association is usually left with a small amount of money, which is used as seed for the next powwow. The association itself is a non-profit organization and must be accountable for its financial operations.

Donors to the Annual Powwow

THE DONORS LISTED BELOW have donated cash or goods or services to the Mankato Powwow at one time or another, and many of them have been making annual donations to the powwow since the very beginning in 1972. Some have been very generous donations, much more than others, but all donations have been important and helpful. The powwow certainly could not have occurred without the help it has received from the business community in the surrounding area and from individual citizens. All this help is surely additional evidence that the reconciliations efforts of all involved have had some success. This help serves to prove once again that the American Indians are welcome in south-central Minnesota. Although this list is long and probably includes most of the businesses in the city of Mankato, it is certainly not exhaustive and is inadvertently likely to have omitted some of the donors who have contributed.

In addition, all the members of the Mdewakanton Association and many of the associates are donors to the powwow. They contribute not only their time and energy going to meetings and helping out at the powwow, but also their cars and trucks for use at the powwow, some traveling many miles to get there, and some burning up a lot of fuel running errands at the powwow. They are not reimbursed for any of their expenses.

In the most general terms, it should be evident from all this that the powwow has had very significant and meaningful support from the local communities and the Indian communities throughout Minnesota and even beyond.

Each year the Mdewakanton Club (also called the Mdewakanton Association or "Powwow Committee") produces a program of events that is given to visitors at the powwow. On the back of the program is listed the businesses and organizations and individuals who donated to that powwow. The following list of donors comes from the randomly selected programs for just two of the powwows (1989 and 1991) that have gone on for nearly four decades. Also, it is certain that there have been many other donors in other years that are not included in the list below. The long list is presented merely to make the point that the community has been very supportive.

All Seasons Tour and Travel
American Banks
American State Bank
American Legion, Kasota
American Red Cross, Mankato
Auto Max
Bamco, Inc. (McDonald's)
Bank of Commerce
Best Western Garden Inn
Bienke, Erma
Blue Earth C'ty. Sheriff's Dept.
Boy Scouts of America
Brady Chiropractic
Brett's Department Store
C & N Sales Amusement
C & S Supply
Carlson Accounting
Carlson Craft
Carlstrom Construction Company
Charlie's Restaurant
Chip Steak and Provision
City of Mankato

City of North Mankato
Coca-Cola Bottling
Cook, Barb
Cotter Company
Country Kitchen, St Peter
Creative Financial Planners
Crooks, Glynn
Darold's Flooring
DeGrood's Appliances
Dick Davis Business Machines
D. M. Stamps and Specialties
Dominos Pizza
Dotson Company, Inc.
Embers Restaurant
Gag's Camper Way
Gislason, Dosland, Hunter, & Malecki
Godfather's Pizza, St Peter
Hacienda Restaurant
Hang-ups
Happy Chef Systems
Hardee's Campus Restaurant
Hardee's West Restaurant

Hiniker Saw Mill
Holsum Bakery
Homeline Furniture, St Peter
Honeymead
Hormel Candy and Tobacco Co.
Hubbard Milling Company
Hy-Vee Food Stores
Independent School District #77
Insight Security
Jim's Sporting Goods
Johnson Fishing, Inc.
Kato Engineering
Kato Sanitation
Kinko Copy Center
Kruger Motors
Lampert Lumber
Landkammers-Johnson-Bowman
LaRoche Rentals
Leighton Swenson Agency, St Peter
Lindsay Sash
Lloyd Lumber Company
Lower Sioux Community, Morton
Lutes Travel
Mankato Bowl
Mankato Citizen's Telephone/Hickory Tech
Mankato Ford
Mankato Free Press
Mankato State University–Cultural Diversity Program
Mankato YMCA
Marigold Dairy
Mayflower Moving
Meyer and Sons
MICO
Mid America Bank
Minority Groups Studies Center, MSU
Morison-Ario VFW

National Poly Products
Nicollet County Bank, St Peter
Northern States Power
Northland Beverage
North Star Concrete
Norwest Bank
Oasis Truck Stop
P.C.A. Credit Analysts
Pepsi Cola
Perkins Restaurant
Prairie Island Sioux Community, Welch, MN
R & R Tire
Randall Foods
Running Moccasin Sioux Community, Iowa
Sally Peters
Sears
Security State Bank
Sentence to Serve
Shakopee Mdewakanton Sioux Com.
Southern Minnesota Construction
Southwest Leasing
St John's Episcopal Church, Mankato
Subway Sandwiches
Superior Concrete
Tastee Bread
Taylor Corporation
Tire Associates
Upper Sioux Com'ty, Granite Falls
Valley National Bank
Valley Optometric Center
Valley Sales and Service
Walter H. Strand VFW #950
Whiskey River Emporium, St Peter
Wilson Trailer Company
Y.M.C.A.
Y.W.C.A.

Chapter Five

Spin-offs from the Powwow

Removal of the Old Stone Marker

IN 1971, THE MANKATO COMMUNITY seemed to have more sensitivity to the issues associated with the Dakota American Indians. There is little doubt that the talks at the Mankato schools by Amos Owen and Vernell and Ernest Wabasha and others, the efforts of Jim Buckley and the Mankato YMCA and its Indian Guide Program, and the efforts of individuals like Bud Lawrence were all having a profound effect on the community. One result was the removal of the stone monument at the site of the hanging of the thirty-eight warriors. It had suffered repeated vandalism over the years, and despite the neutrality of its message it seemed to anger many people. The mayor of Mankato at the time was Vern Lundin. Apparently on his own authority, he had some of the city's maintenance men remove it to a city garage and later bury it under a pile of gravel in a city storage lot. For a time, at least, that seemed to settle the issue of what to do about it.

The New Memorial Plaque

IN NOVEMBER, 1975, A "Memorial Reconciliation Ceremony" was held at a site near where the hotly contested stone hanging marker had been previously located. The Dakota and the Mankato community cosponsored the ceremony, as stated on the plaque, "in an effort to move forward together as one people striving for social change and equality through education and understanding."

The following text is taken directly from the new marker that was subsequently installed on this site in 1976. The Minnesota Historical Society and the Blue Earth County Historical Society erected the new marker. The marker is very much like many other historical markers put in place throughout Minnesota by the

Minnesota Historical Society, and it has little resemblance to the old stone marker that was removed. It consists of a large plaque that displays the following message:

(SIOUX) MEMORIAL—1862

The last act of Minnesota's 1862 Dakota (Sioux) War took place here in Mankato on December 26, 1862, when thirty-eight Dakota American Indians died in a mass execution on this site.

The 1862 War was a culmination of years of friction between the Dakota and whites as settlement pushed into Indian hunting grounds. Government agents and missionaries hoped the Dakota could be taught to live as farmers and worship as Christians, but, as Chief Big Eagle said many years later, "It seemed too sudden to make such a change. . . . If the American Indians had tried to make the whites live like them, the whites would have resisted, and it was the same way with many American Indians." The Minnesota uprising was one of the nation's most costly wars, both in lives lost and property destroyed. It resulted in the near depopulation of the frontier and the exile of the Dakota from Minnesota.

At the war's conclusion, a five-man military commission held trials for several hundred Indian prisoners, and on November 5, 1862, 303 were condemned to death. Henry B. Whipple, Episcopal bishop of Minnesota, talked with President Abraham Lincoln on behalf of the American Indians. After listening to the bishop and personally reviewing the trial records, Lincoln commuted the death sentences of all but thirty-eight prisoners. At 10:00 a.m. on December 26, 1862, the condemned men, chanting the death song, marched in single file to a scaffold guarded by 1,400 troops in full battle dress. A crowd of citizens was on hand to witness the largest mass execution in United States history.

* * *

It is of some interest that the new plaque describes in much more detail the 1862 war, the "trials," and the hanging, thereby giving more foundation to the possibility that some people might find it offensive. Compared with the simple statement of fact on the old marker, the new one contains a lot more information. However, it does not seem to rankle anyone and has not yet been subjected to the kind of vandalism that the old one suffered repeatedly.

* * *

The *Winter Warrior*

Bᴜᴅ Lᴀᴡʀᴇɴᴄᴇ ᴛᴏʟᴅ ᴍᴇ ᴛʜᴇ ɪᴅᴇᴀ for the *Winter Warrior* statue came from sculptor Tom Miller himself. I called Mr. Miller and learned from him that, for a long time, ever since he was a child, he thought there should be some sort of monument near the hanging site that would actually honor the thirty-eight warriors who perished there. All that existed was the old stone marker of the place where they were hanged. He thought about that for a long time and finally, in 1977, he decided that he would try to do something about it. He developed a plan to carve a statue of an Indian warrior to be placed near the site of the hanging. Then he went to the Vetter Stone Company and solicited a donation of stone from which the statue would be carved. That was before he even had talked with the American Indians or any of the other supporters who eventually facilitated the work.

He then drafted specific plans for the statue, made some sketches, and approached the Mdewakanton Club with his ideas. According to Mr. Miller, the club's response was not much more than approving what he was proposing and wishing him, "Good luck," but certain members of the Mdewakanton Club took the proposal under its wing and supported it to the extent that eventually the "Dakota *Winter Warrior* Statue Committee" was established by the City of Mankato's Human Rights Commission. Bruce and Sheryl Dowlin chaired the committee and provided the necessary leadership for the project. Local businesses were solicited for financial support and sufficient support was found. The Mankato City Council minutes of September 28, 1987, and October 5, 1987, reflect approval of a resolution to contribute $2,500 to the Dakota Indian Statue Committee.

A local construction contractor, Don Borneke, who was an acquaintance of Mr. Miller, moved the uncut stone at no cost from the quarry to a farm operated by Mr. Miller's parents near Marysburg, Minnesota. This was no easy task, as the uncut stone weighed several tons, but Mr. Borneke was able to accomplish the job with his construction equipment. Through the next year as he worked on the statue, Mr. Miller consulted with Amos Owen to ensure that everything about the statue was culturally correct. The sculptor was given only nominal commissions, but enough to keep him going. He was a single man then, living at the home of his parents, and he didn't need a lot to sustain him.

The statue was finished and put into place (again by Mr. Borneke) at the Mankato Library in time for the dedication ceremony on December 26, 1987, as part of "The Year of Reconciliation" celebrations. This statue is located across the street from the hanging site.

This statue is located near the intersection of Main and Riverfront Drive in Mankato. (Author's private collection)

Memorial Run on December 26

In 1986, WILLIE MALEBEAR HAD A VISION or dream that was the beginning of the Memorial Run on December 26th, the anniversary of the hanging of the thirty-eight warriors in Mankato. Willie, one of the few remaining American Indians genetically one-hundred-percent Indian, is very proud of his heritage. In the dream he saw himself running in the company of a white man. The dream was somewhat puzzling to him.

At a birthday party for Amos Owen in August 1986 (his seventieth), Willie talked with Amos about the dream. Amos interpreted it as a vision of "some kind of ceremonial run." As they talked, Willie was astonished when he spotted a white man also attending the birthday party. He almost shouted at Amos, "There he is! That's the white man in my dream." Amos then introduced Willie to Bruce Dowlin, who happened to be a marathon runner, and who at that time was also the president of the Mdewakanton Club in Mankato. Bruce was then invited into the discussion and the idea emerged to have a run from Fort Snelling to Mankato to commemorate and honor the thirty-eight warriors who were hanged.

The first Commemorative Run started at Fort Snelling at midnight on December 25th, 1986, following a pipe ceremony. There were thirteen runners including Bruce Dowlin and Willie Malebear. Bruce was the only white guy. One of the other runners was a woman. The event was to be part of the kick off celebration for "The Year of Reconciliation." When the runners arrived at Land of Memories Park the next morning at about the time the hanging happened 125 years earlier, there was a ceremony to honor the thirty-eight who were hanged. As part of the ceremony, the proclamation of Governor Perpich making 1987 "The Year of Reconciliation" was read aloud by Chris Cavender. The commemorative run and the ceremony at the end of it have become an annual event and have taken place every year since 1986.

At midnight on Christmas Day, after all the Christmas festivities are over, there is a gathering of people at Land of Memories Park in Mankato. Actually, the gathering starts before midnight, when some of these people show up around 10:00 p.m. to shovel snow, clearing out a circle of bare ground. By midnight, the circle is ready. It is then blessed by the spiritual leader, or if he is not there a pipe carrier will bless it. A careful arrangement of wood with kindling under it is then completed for the lighting of a spirit fire in the middle of the circle.

At exactly midnight the fire is lit. By that time a small crowd of people have arrived to witness the lighting ceremony, which includes Dakota prayers to make the fire a spiritual one. Some of these people will spend the whole night in or near the circle to attend to the spirit fire. Typically these people fast and focus their attention on the event and the significance of it. Others return in the morning. The fire tenders have the responsibility to spend the night by the fire, keeping the hot fire blazing brightly all night long. The fire serves as a beacon for the runners on their way to this place and to provide spiritual warmth for them as well. Temperatures on December 26th are often near zero.

The runners start out at Fort Snelling, about sixty miles from Mankato, on the river bottom land there, the place where 1,700 American Indians were encamped and spent the winter of 1862-1863. These were all the captured Dakota who had not been hanged or sent to prison following the war of 1862. More than half of them were women and children. Many of them had not participated in the war at all. And yet 200 American Indians died of exposure or malnutrition in that internment camp during that winter. Nearly all of the runners are descendants of those so confined through the winter at that camp.

At Fort Snelling, a pipe ceremony and/or a sweat lodge purification ceremony is held to spiritually prepare the runners for their trek. Then, at midnight, when the spiritual beacon fire is lit at Land of Memories Park in Mankato, the runners at Fort Snelling start out. One of them carries a staff of eagle feathers honoring the thirty-eight who were hanged. At first, all of the participants start out running. Some distance down the road, the run turns into a relay with one of the runners carrying the staff alone or perhaps accompanied by a few of the others. The runners are accompanied by a convoy of cars and trucks carrying all the other runners. Whenever the runner with the staff is exhausted, he is replaced by one of the runners who was resting. This continues the whole distance regardless of the weather, which often has had wind-chill temperatures well below zero, high winds, snow, and icy conditions. More often than not, it is an extremely uncomfortable marathon for most people. The runners endure these conditions willingly, however, sacrificing their personal comfort for the purpose of honoring the thirty-eight hanged.

They arrive in Mankato late in the morning of December 26th, the anniversary of the hanging, and their arrival approximates the time of day when the hanging took place. They pass by the site of the hanging and a prayer is offered as they do. At this point, all the participants are running together through downtown Mankato. They then proceed to Land of Memories Park where the powwow is held each September. By the time they arrive, thirty-eight red willow prayer sticks have been set into the ground and snow around the periphery of the circle. The spiritual fire that has been burning all night continues to burn brightly. A large crowd of more than a hundred people gathers to see the runners arrive and to participate in the prayer ceremony that follows their arrival.

At approximately 11:00 a.m. the crowd is alerted by the sound of drumming in the distance. Then, at a distance of several hundred yards, the runners can be seen approaching, led by the drum group in the back of a pickup truck. The drumming continues as the runners travel four times around the circle and then enter it, stationing themselves around the edge of it. The honor ceremony's spiritual leader and the drum group takes positions inside the circle near the spirit fire, and the ceremony begins with prayers and drumming and songs to honor the thirty-eight warriors. The prayers and songs are offered in the Dakota language. A speaker addresses the crowd with some history and tells the crowd in English about the meaning of this ceremony to the Dakota people.

In recent years the ceremony has been augmented by the arrival of Arvol Lookinghorse's Riders, a group of Dakota on horseback who begin their ride 320 miles west in South Dakota. For the last leg of the ride, they start at the Lower Sioux Reservation near Morton, Minnesota, and converge at Land of Memories Park soon after the runners on foot arrive there (see color plate). Arvol Lookinghorse is the nineteenth generation carrier of the sacred pipe given to the Dakota people by the Buffalo Spirit Woman.

When the honor ceremony is over, there is a feast to celebrate the occasion. For many years food was made available in a building near the circle (the building was the park's machine shed, actually). The food was traditional American Indian food consisting mainly of hot soup and a sandwich, and *wojapi*, a wild berry pudding. This feast continues to be offered, but in more recent years, for those not leaving for home immediately, another meal, the usual church meal, perhaps a turkey dinner instead of traditional American Indian fare, has been made available in a local church.

When the meal at Land of Memories Park is over and the runners and all the visitors have departed, volunteers from the Mdewakanton Association remain to put things away and clean up the area. Everything is neat and tidy when the volunteers leave. On one such occasion I was picking up left-over wood all by myself after the feast. It was late afternoon, and the sun was already low in the crystal-clear, icy-blue winter sky. The sun was shining brightly, but it gave no warmth at all. Nobody else was in sight, though some of the association members still lingered in the park's machine shed where the feast had been held.

Suddenly I heard a very loud, "EEEEEYYIIIIIII!" that seemed to ring in my ears as it came off the top of the hill behind the shed. The way it broke the silence was quite startling. I paused in my work and scanned the hillside trying to see the source of that remarkable sound. I'm very sure it could have been heard at an extremely long distance, perhaps even miles away. But, surprisingly, there was nobody in sight. And there was no other sound except for the whisper of the very slight cold breeze. I returned to my work. After picking up the leftover wood for a supply to be saved for the next vigil fire, I headed for the cook shack to pick up the wood left there. I had just finished doing that, topping off a pretty good pickup load, and I was just about to leave the park to go home when Bob Klanderud, also known as "Bob the Cutter," drove up behind me.

"I'm glad I caught you before you left," he said. "I just wanted to say hello."

"Well, I'm glad you caught me," I replied as I dropped everything and went to shake his hand. "I'm happy to see you. I was looking for you, but then I thought that you were not here."

"I was up on the hill praying," he said.

This event, the commemorative run and vigil fire, had started at midnight that day, but I had not seen Bob until now and it was late in the afternoon, getting dark, and although it was already cold the temperature was dropping. His faded denim pants were wet from the cuffs to well above the knees. In some places there was nearly that much snow, but I imagined he had been kneeling in the snow as he prayed up on the hill. The Dakota consider that hill a sacred place. It is an ancient burial place for the Dakota and there are many tobacco ties on the branches of the trees up there. I presumed that he had been up there fasting, as was his custom at such events, and praying through the night and all day. I was fairly sure the whoop I heard came from him. I thought it might have been his way of greeting me.

A couple of years later at the powwow he visited my camp, and I found opportunity to ask him if he made that loud "whoop" that came from the hill after the commemorative run. He remembered it and acknowledged that it had originated with him.

I asked, "Was that a greeting for me?"

He replied, "Well, it was a greeting, but not just for you. It was for everyone."

He went on to explain that he is an "Akisha," an anointed holy sound maker, one called upon by the spirits to make that sound at certain events. He said that the sound comes from within him, is drawn out of him, but he is not responsible for it.

"I am called upon to do that," he said, adding, "They bring it out of me."

I wasn't sure who "they" were, at first, but it became clear as we talked that he meant "the spirits." The way he talked about it, he was only a channel for this sound.

He said, "It's an ancient sound. Sometimes it's feeble and I am embarrassed by it, but sometimes it is so strong that it cracks the sky."

He went on to say that it is a sacred sound and that many years ago it was used in battle. "It could paralyze the enemy," he said.

I told him that the time I heard it was one time it sounded as if it might have cracked the sky.

When that conversation ended, I watched him for a while as he played with his son. As I might have expected, he was instructive, gentle, persuasive, permissive, and tender. The boy ran to his father to complain that a log had rolled over his leg and broken it. Bob put the boy's leg in a makeshift splint and took him to their car. The boy hobbled to the car with Bob's help. It was apparent that it was only a game, and both seemed to enjoy it. I have always enjoyed knowing Bob and I always find great pleasure talking with him every time we cross paths. I have learned a lot from him.

Land of Memories Park Established

THE PARK WAS DEDICATED by the City of Mankato as "The Dakota Wokiksuye Makoce, meaning "Land of Memories Park" when translated from the Dakota language. The name was recommended by Amos Owen, who was then representing the Dakota communities. This new park has been the locus of the traditional pow-wow since 1980. It is also the location of the commemorative ceremony at the end of the memorial run on December 26th. It is a huge improvement over the old location for the club's events because it has more space, better facilities, much better parking, and more and better camping facilities.

Guy Erickson, a former president of the Mdewakanton Club, worked as head of the grounds crew at the powwow for more than a decade. He reported that in 1972 there were only five bleachers around a seventy-five-foot circle (or arena), there were relatively few concessions, and only one small dumpster was needed to handle all the refuse from the relatively small number of people there. But by 1987, the size of the arena was more than doubled to handle the greater number of dancers, up to hundreds in a single dance, and there were fourteen bleachers for over 3,000 spectators, forty-seven concessions, and several large dumpsters were required to handle the refuse. At times the fourteen bleachers would be fully loaded, with many people left standing around the arena to watch the dancing. The powwow has grown over the years to become a very expansive event, with the powwow events and the campers covering an area of perhaps ten acres. The parking area for several hundred cars covers many more acres. The park is large enough to accommodate all of these requirements.

Within the area of the powwow are many level campsites rented by the city to campers with RVs visiting the Mankato area throughout the camping season. These sites are closed to the general public during the powwow weekend in order to make them available to campers attending the powwow. A large toilet and showering facility is available to the campers. Electricity (within limits) is available to campers and it is provided at no cost during the powwow. Also, there is a large covered shelter, perhaps twenty-by-forty feet, for use in inclement weather. This shelter is used at the powwow as the "cook shack" where communal meals are prepared and served.

In addition, there are waste disposal receptacles, perhaps fifty picnic tables, and several places where potable water can be obtained, all provided by the city at no cost to the powwow. When exiting the park after the powwow, there is a sanitary dump station that campers with RVs can use at no cost. These camp grounds and facilities and the park as a whole are maintained by the City of Mankato. During the powwow, the city does not charge the campers for camping, and the park maintenance personnel are there to aid the powwow wherever necessary. The use of the park for the powwow is a very significant contribution to the powwow that can be counted upon every year from the City of Mankato, and ultimately from the citizens of Mankato.

The Amos Owen Parkette
(Otherwise officially and more widely known as: Reconciliation Park)
(*See* color plate of carved buffalo)

In 1990, A PIECE OF LAND was being sold by the railroad company to the City of Mankato. An article appeared in the *Mankato Free Press* about the sale. The land was near Veteran's Memorial Bridge and the city was paying about twenty thousand dollars for it.

When Bud Lawrence read the news article he thought, "I wonder if that land is close to the site where the thirty-eight Dakota were hanged, and I wonder what the city's going to do with it."

This was sufficiently interesting to Bud that he made some inquiries and learned that, in fact, the land in question was the precise location where the thirty-eight Dakota had been hanged in 1862.

Then questions arose regarding, "What would the city do with this land? Was it going to be a building site? A parking lot? Were plans already established for it?" Some possibilities for what might be developed there might even be degrading to the fact that this property was the site of an incredibly important historical event that took place there in 1862.

More inquiries revealed that there were no established plans for this piece of property. That left open the possibility of setting aside that land as a city park, and Bud drew up a proposal for the city manager, Bill Bassett, to consider. He thought that a park in that location was a good idea. He took the idea to the City Council and they approved it.

A review of the minutes of the Mankato City Council reveals that immediately after the death of Amos Owen on June 4, 1990, the council had already considered doing something to honor him for his reconciliation efforts. At a regular council meeting on June 11, 1990, less than a week after Amos died, there was discussion leading to the recommendation that the Human Rights Commission should establish a committee for this purpose. In a subsequent meeting on May 13, 1991, the recommendation coming from that committee that "a reconciliation park be established in honor of Amos Owen" was approved unanimously by the council.

The park committee that was established drew up specific plans for the park. The members of this committee are listed as the park "Founders" on a bronze plaque now located in the park, as reproduced below:

Hereditary Chief Ernest Wabasha and his wife, Vernell
Mankato Mayor Stanley Christ
Louis G. "Bud" Lawrence, co-chairman
James H. Buckley Sr., co-chairman
Jim Peterson
Jeffrey Kagermeier, A.I.A.
Bruce and Sheryl Dowlin
Perry Wood
Thomas M. Miller, Sculptor

Perhaps Bill Bassett, the Mankato city manager, should have been listed there too. His help at the start certainly was instrumental in getting the whole park idea off the ground and approved by the city council. He was subsequently honored at the powwow for his role in getting the park established. He was given an honor blanket and an honor dance was held for him. He had to be coaxed to get into the arena and dance in his own honor dance.

The park committee struggled for a long time with making plans for the park. Bud Lawrence wanted to name the park "The Amos Owen Parkette" and for a long time, for most of the seven years that the planning continued, that was what the park was called. But there was opposition to this name for the park. Many thought that it would be wrong to name the park for Amos, though they all acknowledged that Amos was clearly deserving of much recognition for the work that he had done in his lifetime. Eventually they settled upon "Reconciliation Park" to commemorate the broader meaning of the park, the repair of the relationships between the American Indian communities and the local communities to which the Dakota had for so long felt unwelcome. The name clearly diverts the focus of the park away from the hanging that took place there. With this name, the focus of the park is almost opposite in direction. "Reconciliation" connotes the establishment of peace and harmony between oppositional factions. That is what the park is intended to commemorate. With recognition of the humility that Amos Owen was well known to have had, and with the importance that Amos placed upon the whole idea of reconciliation, it is absolutely certain that he would have approved of the final decision for the name of this important park.

Reconciliation Park is now a reality. The park was dedicated in a ceremony attended by most of the people involved in developing it. The ceremony was held on September 21, 1997, in conjunction with the annual powwow. The planning committee did a wonderful job. It is a place where visitors can find peace and harmony, where they can relax and reflect on not only the events of the horrible war and its consequences that took place here, but also on the recent peaceful social reparations that the park represents. Why is the sixty-five-ton Kasota stone carved buffalo there? Vernell Wabasha suggested it in one of the planning meetings because of the importance of the buffalo to the Dakota people. It represents the presence of the Dakota people in this still largely white community. It says, "The Dakota have come back," and it says that in a beautiful and friendly way. There is harmony in the shrubs and trees selected for planting there. The trees are Sioux land cottonwood trees. And the park is still developing so that, in the future, flowers and sweet grass and sage might be added.

The large buffalo in Reconciliation Park was carved out of a sixty-seven-ton Kasota stone block by Thomas M. Miller, the same sculptor who carved the *Winter Warrior* statue across the street from the park. (*See* color plate.) The park and the buffalo are located on the site of the 1862 hanging of the thirty-eight Dakota warriors. The carved buffalo became a reality as the result of collaborative efforts of Dakota and white communities.

Donors for Reconciliation Park

Dakota Tribes cash donations $71,510.00
Firefly Creek Casino, Upper Sioux Community, Minnesota
Devils Lake Sioux Community, North Dakota
Lower Sioux Community, Minnesota
Prairie Island Sioux Community, Minnesota
Shakopee Sioux Community, Minnesota
Sisseton-Wahpeton Sioux Community, South Dakota
Mankato Community Cash Donations $2725.00
Anonymous MICO
Brad Buscher Norwest Bank
Carol Hannick JC Penny

In-kind Contributions (Approximate monetary value) $100,000.00

George Carlstrom Construction Company (Rocks for foundation)
Robert Carlstrom Construction Company (Rocks for foundation)
Diversity Foundations
City of Mankato (Park land, planted Sioux land cottonwood trees)
City of North Mankato
Fisher and Hoehn Electric, Inc.
Graybar Electric Co. (Floodlights)
H & C Electric/Graybar (Floodlights)
Kagermeier, Skaar, Paulsen & Asleson Architects, Inc. (Blueprints)
Al Klinkhammer (Painted signs)
Lloyd Lumber Co. (Plywood for signs)
Minnesota Valley Regional Library
North Star Concrete Co. (Concrete foundation)
Shane Cohen Landscape Architects (Planning)
Southern Minnesota Const. Co. (Hauled stone from the quarry)
Spring Green Inc.
Terratron, Inc.
The motor shop (Installed the lighting)
Vetter Stone Co. (Reduced price for the sixty-seven-ton stone)

Amos Owen's Prayer

Grandfather, I come to you this day
In my humble way to offer my prayers
For the thirty-eight Dakota who perished
In Mankato in the year of 1862.
To the West I pray to the Horse Nation

And to the North I pray to the Elk People.
To the East I pray to the Buffalo Nation
And to the South I pray to the Spirit People.
To the Heavens I pray to the Great Spirit
And to the Spotted Eagle.
And Below I pray to Mother Earth
To help us in this time of reconciliation.
Grandfather, I offer these prayers in my humble way
To all my relatives.

Though at the time of the dedication of Reconciliation Park (September 21, 1997), Amos Owen had already passed away (June 4, 1990), his prayer was a part of the dedication ceremony. The prayer was written more than seven years before the dedication of Reconciliation Park, but it appears that even then he knew it would happen.

Chapter Six

Mahkato Education Day Project

(1987 to 2011)

THIS CHAPTER WAS CO-WRITTEN with Dr. Sheryl Dowlin and her husband, Bruce. Sheryl was a professor at Mankato State University and is the author of many academic papers about reconciliation, the Mankato Powwow, and the Education Day project at the Mankato Powwow. The material for this chapter includes the Dowlins's first-hand accounts, cited reference materials (with their permission) from unpublished researched articles, brochures and published journal articles written by the Dowlins about the Reconciliation efforts between the Dakota and other tribal groups and non-American Indians. The annual Mahkato Education Day project is held in conjunction with the Mankato Powwow. The Dowlins, with guidance from members of the Prairie Island Mdewakanton Dakota Community (namely Amos and Ione Owen) and the Mankato School District served as coordinators for the first Mankato third-grade Education Day project in 1987. These primary entities continued to work together for fourteen years, until the Dowlins retired from their responsibilities in 2000 at which time Paul and Vicky Barry took the Dowlins's place. The Dowlins's responsibilities included serving as liaisons between the Dakota and Mankato communities, fundraising, logistic setup, record keeping, and in later years resource staff recruitment. Amos and Ione Owen provided the necessary spiritual and cultural guidance in the design of the event and the recruitment of the first Dakota and other tribal member resource staff. Mankato School District #77 provided funding and logistical work for the transportation of all school district third graders to and from the Education Project site, Land of Memories Park. The school district was also instrumental in the design of the project from the school district's perspective. They requested two one-and-one-half-hour sessions (morning and afternoon), required small learning circles (twelve to fifteen children) staffed by a native resource person. As the third-grade student population grew over the years, more learning stations and resource staff were added.

In 2001, Paul and Vicky Barry, long-time Education Day resource staff and members of the Mdewakanton Club, picked up the liaison mantle and continued in that capacity until 2010. In 2011, a Dakota woman, Ramona Stately, from the Mdewakanton Shakopee community, became the new liaison for the project.

At the end of the Dowlin tenure in 2000, Sheryl completed her fourteen-year longitudinal study of the project outcomes and produced a video documentary all of the 2000 Education Day project activities. In 2012, the Mahkato Education Day project will celebrate its twenty-fifth "new ceremony" anniversary carrying on the challenge issued by Vine Deloria, Jr. in 1987 to bring Natives and non-natives together with the land on a repetitive basis. Vine Deloria, Jr. was a nationally known American Indian theologian, historian, educator, and Indian activist.

Prior to 1987, as far back as the 1960s and long before the first 1972 Dakota-Mankato Powwow took place, Dakota people came to Mankato Schools to educate school children about their history and culture. Members of the Owen family, Norman and Edith Crooks and their son Glynn, Vernell and Ernest Wabasha (see Color Plate Five), and Harvey and Bertha Davenport provided educational opportunities for the children in the Mankato schools for many years before 1972. They visited schools and presented educational programs on a regular basis in classroom and auditorium settings. These efforts, coordinated by Bud Lawrence and Jim Buckley, proved meaningful to both students and teachers. They continued visiting the Mankato schools until the redesigned Education Day project working exclusively with third graders was initiated in 1987. Third graders were chosen for the project by Mankato School District Superintendent Bob Nelson because Mankato History was studied at that grade level and because third graders did not have an equal number of field trips as the sixth graders did.

The third-grade children, their teachers, and parent chaperones enjoyed the person to person time; meeting, talking with, and learning from many different members of the Dakota and other tribal communities. Native resource staff persons offered direct, unique and personal learning experiences listening first hand to Native resource staff members' stories about their culture. They observed Native craftspersons make moccasins, flutes, regalia, drums, and other items in real time and through one-on-one interactions discovered many common interests in sports, vocations and hobbies.

In those first few years of the project, the textbooks used in schools perpetuated stereotypes and misinformation about Dakota history and culture. This misinformation served to widen the gap of understanding and acceptance of the Dakota people and other tribal members. Meeting American Indian people as people in these unique educational situations proved to be more meaningful to the children and their teachers than just reading about people and these things in books. Reports from parents and teachers indicated some of the children overcame their fears of native people when they met them and learned from them in this context. For many children, those fears had been nurtured by cowboy-and-Indian movies and stories they had heard. Their experiences at the Mahkato Education Day dispelled many of those inaccuracies about the Dakota and other tribal members.

The educational efforts coordinated by the Dakota, the Mankato School District and the Mankato Community at-large with the help of the Dowlins were well received by school administrators, teachers, children, and their parents. Over time, friendships were established between teachers and native resource people who came every year. These developing relationships contributed to a recognition by the Dakota, Mankato School administrators, and Mankato community members of the importance of this "new ceremony" project in helping to bridge the gap of misunderstanding between cultures. As a benefit of these cross-cultural relationships, and the superb lessons offered by the dedicated native resource people, the way was paved for this project to become recognized as an integral and valuable part of the school curriculum.

The history of the redesigned Education Day third-grade project emerged in August 1987 as a follow-up concept to the state-wide reconciliation work begun in December 1986, in anticipation of the 125th anniversary of the Dakota War. Governor Rudy Perpich issued a proclamation declaring 1987 as the Year of Reconciliation between Minnesotans and the Dakota people. This declaration precipitated several special educational events in 1987 that furthered the cause of reconciliation.

During that year, Bruce Dowlin, as president of the Mdewakanton Club and his wife, Sheryl, traveled countless miles throughout Minnesota representing the Mdewakanton Club at events. Halfway through that year, they emerged from one of those events inspired with an idea that was the initiation of the Mahkato Education Day project held on the powwow grounds during the 1987 Mankato Powwow. This project started independent of the support of the Mdewakanton Club. Several members felt strongly the club should only be about the business of putting on a powwow. Despite opposition from these club members, the first annual Education Day project became a reality that took place in conjunction with the powwow, but it was not viewed as a part of the powwow at that time and for several years to follow by leaders in the Mdewakanton Club. The project proved worthwhile as an important part of Mankato third-graders' education thanks to the devoted members of the Dakota and other tribal communities who came every year to serve as resource people.

In the conceptualization stage, the Dowlins had in mind a field trip for Mankato sixth graders to go to the site where the carving of the *Winter Warrior* statue was under way. They presented their idea to the District #77 Superintendent of Schools Bob Nelson, who said that there was no way to bus the sixth-graders to the site as it was too far away. However, Nelson was interested in some kind of field trip for third-graders to Land of Memories Park during the September three-day powwow activities located only a few miles from the local schools. He suggested that the Friday before the powwow began would be a good time for it. Bruce and Sheryl traveled to Prairie Island to discuss the proposal with Amos Owen and his wife, Ione, who were enthusiastic about doing it and immediately offered suggestions for the design of it and identified the names of Dakota and other tribal people who would be invited to teach the children and their teachers.

The first Mahkato Education Day took place on the Friday of the 1987 Powwow weekend with less than two months of preparation. Everyone involved worked hard to get it organized and ready to be implemented in that short amount of time. The educational format for the project was developed by the Mankato School District superintendent and the resource people doing the presentations at the learning stations were selected and contacted by Amos and Ione Owen and Tom Goldtooth. Without their generous efforts, the project probably would not have happened.

Based upon the number of third-graders attending and the school district's request for small learning groups, thirteen learning stations were set up in the large grassy area adjacent to the powwow grounds. Half of the third-graders were to be bussed out to the park for the morning session and the other half were scheduled for an afternoon session. The Mankato School District arranged for and funded the transportation of them to and from the project site, the Land of Memories Park. Approximately 300 children would participate in the thirteen interactive learning station sessions offered.

Everything was ready to go after all that laborious preparation, but the morning first session had to be cancelled due to rain. Amos, as always, remained positive that things would work out. The Education Committee members experienced a great deal of nervousness because the Mankato School officials had approved this project on a one-year trial basis. It had to prove itself this first time to be considered a second year. Despite the morning session cancellation the Native resource people were there, some having traveled long distances to get to the powwow early so they could engage in this activity. The morning outdoor activity simply could not be done in the rain, and there was no "Plan B."

Despite the cancellation of the morning session, the resource staff people stayed and were ready in case it cleared off in time for the afternoon session. By noon, the rain stopped, the sun shone and the afternoon session was held as scheduled. The teachers who accompanied the children to the afternoon session and the school officials who witnessed it all rated the activity as well-organized and a very good hands-on learning experience for the children and their teachers. From that year forward, the Mankato School District has committed its teachers and resources in support of the continuance of this third-grade education field trip.

That the first Education Day activities were actually completed at all in that first year was described by Sheryl Dowlin as "a wonder." Unexpectedly, the proposed project was met with stiff resistance from some members of the Mdewakanton Club who felt the only responsibility the club should have was to put on the powwow. Had it not been for the determination of Bruce and Sheryl Dowlin and Erma and Marion Beinke (the Education Committee of the Mdewakanton Club), the strong support of Amos and Ione Owen, the leadership of Tom Goldtooth, the participating native resource people and other Dakota community members, the Education Day project might never have become reality. Tom Goldtooth deserves special mention in this context because, along with the help of Amos and Ione Owen, he did an excellent job of recruiting native resource staff for that day. Tom went from tent to tent, waking people to ask them to help out until there were thirteen resource people to staff the thirteen learning stations laid out the first year. Tom committed four years to help out with the project. One couple came to help because Amos and Ione asked for their help. That couple came every year to work as resource staff at two different learning stations (moccasin and flute making) for fifteen years. Another couple traveled from Topeka, Kansas, for as many or more years to serve as resource staff for two additional learning stations (childrens' games). The Dowlins are deeply indebted to each couple's dedication and generosity of time and talents.

The following is a brief description of the design of the Education Day Project and how it works:

Education Day activities are held in a large open grassy field bordered on two sides by a strip of trees along the Minnesota River. The learning stations are set up on Thursday afternoon, the day before Education Day. The learning circle has grown significantly since the first year with thirteen learning stations. In 2011, as many as forty learning stations were placed in a large circle, perhaps a hundred yards in diameter. By Friday morning everything is in place for the arrival of many school busses bringing hundreds of third-graders and their teachers to this event. After all the children have arrived, the day begins with an "Opening Circle" ceremony conducted by a Dakota elder with the children and teachers gathered around him in the middle of the circle. This is their first introduction to the Dakota way of acknowledging the Creator.

At the end of the opening ceremony each class of children is directed to their assigned learning station. There are ten to fifteen children in each group. For twelve minutes, each group is told about and shown aspects of American Indian culture, craftsmanship, and life. The children are often invited to touch or hold hand-made items and given opportunities to ask the resource staff person questions. Then, a car horn blows a signal, and the children are encouraged to thank the resource staff member, shake their hand and move on in a clockwise direction to the next learning station.

All of the children visit between four to six different learning stations. There isn't sufficient time for the groups to visit all stations. Each learning station might feature one or more of the following topics and/or demonstrations: story telling, pipe-making, moccasin-making, flute-making, head roach-making, pottery-making, drum-making, jingle dress-making, traditional men's regalia, men's grass dance regalia, Dakota legends, growing and using corn, tepee living and tepee building, dancing, dream catchers, moccasin game, leather work, ceremonial use of tobacco, children's games, flint knapping/tool making, drumming and songs, or the Dakota language. Topics might change from year to year, and this list is certainly not exhaustive of possible topics.

The success and importance of this project is no longer questioned. It is a valued and important part of the Mankato School District curriculum and third-grader's cultural experiences. It is seen by native resource staff as a safe and unique opportunity to share their culture and their history. Mankato children and teachers for over twenty years have come to appreciate and respect the native culture, and friendships have been formed. On a larger scale, as a benefit of this project, a good percentage of attitudes have been shaped in positive ways towards more realistic perceptions of American Indians, their culture, and their contributions to the Mankato community.

The first years working on this project were a challenge, to say the least. Reasons why club members resisted providing any financial support initially have never been clearly determined. Resistance is often the case when someone or something new is introduced into a well-established organization. Some members were of the opinion that putting on the powwow was sufficient by itself. Most club members seemed to miss the connection between the educational project outcomes and its relationship towards the building of personal and professional relationships within the Mankato community, a community that, over the years, has come to support the powwow in many significant ways.

The first year of the Mahkato Education Day project (1987) was a success despite the fact there were no moneys available for honorariums to help with gas or food for those who traveled long distances or to make copies of instructional materials shared by the native resource staff with teachers. Members of the Mdewakanton Club refused to contribute towards the project for a number of years.

Because of the resistance by club members to support the Education Day project financially or in any other way, a variety of avenues were explored to find needed financial support and volunteers willing to help set up the grounds for the learning day during the first several years. Grants were written, many of which were awarded. The Minnesota Humanities Commission, a grantor, became a strong advocate for the project for many years until their funding ran out. Local service organizations were solicited and made contributions. Individual families made contributions in the memory of a loved one.

One unfortunate miscommunication occurred the third or fourth year Sheryl Dowlin was seeking financial resources to support the education project. She reported: One day while listening to the radio in her car, she tuned into a program that had a Dakota guest from Prairie Island on their show. The guest talked about education grant moneys being available from the tribe for Dakota-related education projects. So, as any fund raiser would do, Sheryl submitted a grant proposal asking for a sum of money to help fund the Education Day Project. The grant was awarded. Unbeknown to Sheryl, her request was apparently assumed by the grantor to be the annual request for the Mankato Powwow funds. As a result of a mistaken assumption, the club did not receive the expected annual funds from that source for the powwow. This situation caused a long-standing resentment towards the education project and Sheryl, specifically, who naively thought the grant award came from a separate Prairie Island Education Grant Fund. Despite this set back, the club managed to find the financial support needed to meet its expenses that year.

By the second year of the Education Day project, the outdoor learning circle was enlarged to include more learning stations to accommodate smaller groups of twelve to fifteen children for each station, thus providing more person-to-person interaction between the children and the native resource staff. The weather was more cooperative, and the resource persons were minimally compensated for expenses with a small honorarium.

In December 1987, Vine Deloria, Jr. was the keynote speaker at the 1987 Treaty Symposium, H.H. Humphrey Institute of Public Affairs in Minneapolis. The concept of reconciliation was the focus of his address. At that time, the dust from the September Mankato Powwow and the very first Education Day had barely settled. In his talk, he said that reconciliation would be difficult and required a "different and a new creative set of ceremonial activities." In the most general of terms he suggested, "A ceremony that when you enter it you give up presuppositions, bad feelings, and assumptions and simply try to have a common experience." And he emphasized that reconciliation is easy to talk about, but it is harder to do. For the Dowlins, his words issued a challenge.

The Dowlins, Erma Bienke, Marion Lichtenberg, and a few other people who had worked on the first Education Day project, envisioned the Education Day project as being one of the "new ceremonies" Deloria talked about—a ceremony that included the land, American Indians and non-American Indians—a ceremony that reoccurred. The land was Land of Memories Park—a spiritual site for the Dakota, the location of the annual Mankato Powwow; the Dakota people and other tribal members; and the Mankato non-Indian children, teachers, school administrators and parents associated with the Mankato School District. Seeing parallels of the Mahkato Education Day project to Deloria's challenge gave more impetus to continue to work to make the Mahkato Education Day an annual "new ceremony" event, held in conjunction with the Mankato Powwow on the site of the powwow grounds in Land of Memories Park.

The Mdewakanton Club's small Education Committee had meetings with school officials and representatives of Dakota communities in Minnesota, Canada, and elsewhere to discuss the continuance of offering the Education Day. Support was given from each entity. This project has continued to be offered on an annual basis for twenty-four years as of 2011. The year 2012 will mark the twenty-fifth anniversary of this ceremony that continues to include the land, Native and non-native people on an annual basis.

Gradually, through all the intervening years, members of the Mdewakanton Club have become more accepting and willing to work cooperatively to maintain the continuance of the Education Day. Now it seems to be an accepted part of the powwow as the original Education Committee had hoped it would be. This outcome is not surprising given the fact that the project has been extremely successful in helping to bridge some of the gaps of understanding between cultures and seems to have contributed to stronger reciprocal relationships on multiple levels—personally, professionally and financially. Such outcomes in terms of a greater understanding and appreciation for one another are indeed examples of reconciliation at work.

In 2000, her last year as a liaison person for the project, Sheryl Dowlin completed a longitudinal study of the impact of Education Day on the Mankato community and relationships between Native and non-native people involved in this project. Her final report was put in the form of a videotaped documentary entitled "Mahkato Education Day: A Conciliatory Ceremony," featuring each of the resource staff personnel in attendance that year and their learning station activities. A faculty research grant from Mankato State University and a grant from the Minnesota Humanities Commission funded this project. Copies of the documentary have never been sold. Rather they have been distributed widely free of charge to schools and libraries in the United States and Canada, and to each child, teacher, administrator, parent, and resource staff member in the production.

Because of its success in Mankato, the Mahkato Education Day project has been replicated in other areas of Minnesota and other parts of the United States. This documentary includes interviews with native resource staff persons, participating children, teachers, parents, and school administrators. The results revealed, "A stronger sense of community has developed between Dakota, other tribal members and Mankato community members as a long-time benefit of this project. There is evidence that a uniting of persons in a spirit of respect and appreciation has occurred." Additional results demonstrated lasting positive perceptions of Dakota and other tribal peoples by children who went through the Education Day field trip experience. Lasting positive perceptions of native people were also evident in the reported friendships developed between Mankato School District teachers and Dakota and other tribal member resource staff individuals. There was also evidence that children who experienced the project became sensitive to others using stereotypes and misinformation. One example was a child who had gone to Education Day in the third grade, correcting her sixth-grade teacher comments about the Dakota history in Minnesota.

The comments from participants are proof positive that Education Day has been a great success. Excerpts from a selection of those comments, as recorded in the year 2000, are available below:

Comments of Resourse Persons

Mike Ballard (N. Cherokee, former Mdewakanton Club president, and a resource person since the beginning): "We feel so strongly about it [Education Day] that we borrowed it for our powwow down in Topeka, Kansas, where we've just completed our eighth Education Day, which is a carbon copy of the one here in Mankato."

Colin Wesaw (Potawatomi/Mohawk): "Every group that I've had this year and in the past have gotten up and shook my hand, and I didn't have to ask them. The teacher didn't tell them. And sometimes one of the kids would come up and tell you how much it meant for them. And you could feel it. You know what I mean?"

Jeanne Boutain Croud (Ojibwe): "The community has been wonderful. The teachers have been so responsive. Teachers will come up to you at the powwow afterwards and say, 'I saw you and you did a wonderful job.' It makes you feel like you did something worthwhile."

Harlan Whipple (Dakota): "The teaching is giving my spirit and my soul to the young kids. . . . We're trying to teach them that life is one big happy family."

Herb Bibeau (Ojibwe): "It's like being a father again when we come down here watching these children grow up. Everyone has a question. You know they're thinking. This is what makes it interesting to teach."

Roger Trudell (Dakota): "I found it pretty interesting that it gave the opportunity for Indian people to let the education system know that we are still in existence and that we were not just a part of history and gone."

Kermit Frazier (Dakota): "I've had a lot of children say they are coming back the next day with their family, and that feels good to know that we're narrowing those wounds—bringing both cultures together again." He also said, "I'd like to see this keep going—the learning and the teaching and the combining of the two nations together. . . . The children are the future, and if we can come together by teaching the positives of both cultures, I think we'll have a better civilization in the future."

Kevin Tacan (Dakota from Sioux Valley in Canada): "It's as if going through all of this every year in the past, how many years you've been doing this, has made a big difference. I can see it in the city. When I drive around, the people are very friendly, very nice. [They show] a lot of respect. [I'll] have a lot of people smiling at me when I am going through the stores."

Paul Berry (Ute): "There's been a lot of positive feedback. We are very lucky to do this in Mankato. There are many communities who couldn't do it for a variety of reasons."

Dottie Whipple (Dakota): "Just a half hour to an hour of teaching people makes a world of difference. . . . Thank you for letting me have a part in this. Thank you."

Comments of School Officials and Teachers

Dave Dakken (associate superintendent, School District #77): "What is so good about this is the fact that it is a real-life experience for kids. . . . They get to take part in the activities out there and so it is so much more than just reading out of a book or seeing pictures or films . . ."

Peg Jeffers (principal, Hoover Elementary School): ". . . we have to limit the number of field experiences the kids can have and so we always have to make a judgment as to which ones are valuable and which ones are not. . . . This is one of the experiences they don't want to lose."

Roberta Barrtoldi (Monroe Elementary third-grade teacher who attended Education Day for fourteen years): "I realized from the get go that these people had their heart and their soul in this activity. . . . These people came from long distances, and they came early in order to be there and connect with the children. So it wasn't just a casual experience. It was well-planned and organized and well worth the effort. There were so many wonderful stations."

Comments from the Kids

Erica Wessbecker (third-grade participant): "Well, it's kind of cool . . . they kind of united everybody, American Indian and white people, and made us see how they kind of survived and what they do, their way of life and how we should respect that. I think it's important because nobody needs to think that they aren't as good as anybody else. We're all people, so I don't see why we can't all be friends."

Emily Waterston (a university student in 2001 when interviewed, participated as a third-grader in 1989): "When you learn in the classroom you learn about the customs and the traditions and the things that are associated with being American Indian. But being out there, you are actually with them. You learn well. They're not always dressed in those clothes, and they don't live in tepees. It gives you a real perspective on how they really are, and I think that is what we need to realize. They are not that different from us. Nothing compares to hands-on learning.

The Mazakute Host Drum Group is playing for a flag raising ceremony to start the day. Eleven drummers can be counted. The American flag, Canadian flag, and a Prisoner of War flag are raised. (Author's private collection)

Photo of Amos Owen (taken by Bud Lawrence) from an article that appeared in the *Today* magazine, a publication of Mankato State University in 2009, almost ten years after Amos passed away. (Courtesy of Bud Lawrence)

The founders, Bud Lawrence, Amos Owen, and Jim Buckley

One of the riders, Richard Milda, at the Commemorative Run in December. (Author's private collection)

The author next to the buffalo at Reconciliation Park. (Author's private collection)

Ernest Wabasha, hereditary chief of the Mdewakanton Dakota, as he might have appeared before school children in his educational efforts. (Courtesy of Bud Lawrence)

Amos Crooks dancing at a Powwow. Note the Seventh Cavalry patch on his shield. Amos served fifteen years in the U. S. Army including three tours of duty in the Korean War in the Seventh Cavalry which was also, ironically, General George Armstrong Custer's outfit at his last stand. (from a memorial poster: IN MEMORY OF AMOS L. CROOKS JULY 25, 1919 TO JULY 13, 1999)

Flag bearers start to enter the arena to begin the Grand Entry. (Author photo)

The Honor Guard follows the initial flag bearers. (Author photo)

After the flags, the men enter in their varied regalia. (Author photo)

And then the Traditional Women enter. (Author photo)

The Royalty, Princesses from various Powwows, enter as a group. (Author photo)

Then come the jingle Dress Dancers. (Author photo)

A Grass Dancer, Russell Harjo, came to the Powwow from Oklahoma. (Author photo)

Emmett Eastman, dancing in Traditional Men's regalia. He is getting old, but he is still very light on his feet and it is a pleasure to watch him dance. He is also a marathon runner who has crossed all the continents around the world on foot. (Author photo)

A Fancy Dancer at the evening dance. (Author photo)

A fancy shawl dancer. (Author photo)

Leslie Walking Elk, Women's Traditional dancer who supervised the cook shack in 2011. (Author photo)

John and Dianne Shoemaker have attended all the Powwows in Mankato since the very beginning. (Author photo)

The author's camp at the Powwow in 2005. (Author photo)

Chapter Seven

Integral Parts of the Powwow

THE AUTHOR IS NOT A DRUMMER, singer, dancer, or expert in any way regarding drumming, singing and dancing at the powwow. However, no book about a powwow could be written without an attempt to describe these activities in some detail because they are such integral parts of powwows. A determined effort was made to glean from books and Internet websites the best information obtainable about all of these things, and some of those sources were quite obscure but nevertheless very informative. For example, the best resource for a description of the various dances at the Mankato Powwow was an unpublished pamphlet entitled "Mah-kato Traditional *Wacipi*" written and produced by the Mdewakanton Club in 1996. Large parts of the following descriptions of dances come directly from that booklet. However, despite the use of the best resources, what follows is, in large part, the knowledge the author has personally acquired through first-hand observation and questioning participants at the Mankato Powwow over a period of the last twenty years.

The *Wacipi* (Dance)

THE MUSIC, INSTRUMENTS, SONGS, dances, and ceremonies of today are very different from those of the early nineteenth century. Samuel Pond came to Minnesota in 1834 with his brother, Gideon, to serve as a Christian missionary to the American Indians. He lived with them for more than twenty years and later wrote a book about their culture and traditions. He described the dance drums as being smaller than they are today, a deer hide stretched over the end of a powder keg, and he said it was beaten with a single stick. He had very little good to say about the Dakota music. "They had popular tunes, some of which were probably very ancient, but no songs except a very few had words which were repeated when the songs were sung. . . . If the Dakotas had any poetry, it was not in songs."[1]

There were several different instruments used by the Dakota to make music, including drums, flutes, whistles, and rattles, but the drum was the most powerful of these because it was believed to convey the heart beat of the world. It provided the rhythm and pace for all the dances.

The Drums

THE MANKATO POWWOW USUALLY has had between fifteen and twenty drums present at the powwow in one weekend. Each of the drums at the Mankato Powwow might represent a different community of American Indians attending the powwow. One or two of these will be the "host drums" selected to be the official drums at the powwow. They have the responsibility of drumming for the main ceremonies, such as the grand entries and the opening and closing ceremonies. However, all of the drums that show up at a powwow are given an opportunity to perform.

The term "drum" is sometimes used to describe the instrument itself, and sometimes it refers to the instrument plus the whole group of men—as many as eight or ten—who are drumming and singing with it. Women are not allowed to be drummers, but they may be a part of the drum group and are often seen standing nearby to participate in the singing.

The drum is considered to have a life or spirit of its own. It is said to have the heartbeat of the Indian Nation and Mother Earth. The drum sounds have healing abilities and other effects on the listeners, putting them in better harmony with the earth and with their souls. Usually a drum is blessed and given the respect of a sacred object. Ancient drums were quite different from those used today. Sometimes the drum was a hollow log, ritualistically painted or otherwise adorned in one way or another, beaten by one or more drummers with sticks.[2]

There are different kinds of drums, including small hand drums used in some ceremonies such as a purification sweat, but at the dancing arena the powwow drum is very much like the common bass drum seen in many marching bands. In fact, sometimes it is precisely such a bass drum, commercially manufactured, possibly purchased and donated to a drum group, but in that case it will likely be modified to have the appearance of an American Indian drum handmade from scratch. The most valued drums are those made from scratch by the drum group or someone in the group.

There are many ways to make a drum. It can vary in its diameter but usually is the approximate size of a common bass drum. The shape of the drum can be round or it might be octagonal. The width of the hoop to which the covers are tied can also vary so that some drums are taller or shorter than others. The hoop is usually made of wood, but some drums have been made from a powder keg or from a section of a steel barrel. The cover very tightly stretched over both the top and bottom of the drum can be made of buffalo hide, cowhide, horse hide, elk skin, or the hide of other game animals. The quality of the cover does have some effect on the tone of the drum, and the tautness of the cover greatly affects the tone. Even the temperature and humidity of the air can have an effect by making the drum cover more or less tightly stretched. On a cool evening, a drum group might be seen warming its drum by the side of a fire. One can hear the tone of an occasional beat change as the drum cover warms and becomes more resonant.

Usually eight drummers encircle the drum. They beat the drum with durable covered mallets that resemble a cattail on a long stem like might be seen at the shore of a pond or lake. The drummers and the lead singer are responsible for knowing a variety of songs so they can satisfy whatever request is made of them.

Upon hearing an American Indian drum group for the first time, a spectator might not be able to distinguish one drum group from another. They might all sound like eight guys sitting around the drum beating on it in unison. But learning to be a drummer takes practice, and drumming has many nuances and many different songs to be learned. Learning to appreciate the skills and talents that go into the drumming, and the different qualities of the drums, also takes some practice listening to the various beats and cadences and tones generated. After listening carefully over time, it becomes easy to recognize the differences in pace, rhythm, and quality of the different drums and drum songs.

Amos Crooks is quoted as having said, on his way once again to the circle to dance, "I thought I was tired from dancing but the drum said I wasn't." The drums talk to the people. (*See* Color Plate Six: Amos Crooks in regalia)

The Songs

Every tribe of American Indians usually has its own song. They are like individual school songs. A song could represent a tribe, clan, family, or any other kind of group membership. Even an individual might have a song representing him- or herself. A Dakota warrior is supposed to have his own death song. The Mankato

Powwow does have its own grand entry song, despite the fact that the powwow does not belong to any one tribe or clan or group. No Indian reservations are located in or near Mankato, but the Mazakute drum group composed a song for the Mankato Powwow's grand entry ceremony. The Mankato Powwow is said to be an "all nations powwow," which means that any tribe from anywhere can attend and participate in it. In fact, participants come from many surrounding states and Canada, and visitors from all over the world have attended it. People from all over the United States and Canada come regularly. However, in addition to the grand entry song, perhaps the Mankato Powwow should have its own reconciliation song because of its special function as a reconciliation powwow. That is something that should and most likely will be developed.

Every drum group will have one or more songs of its own, composed and written by one or more of the group members. Such songs are usually very personal, representing something specific about the drum group or individuals within it and is sung in the language or dialect of the group that created it. However, many standard and traditional songs are performed for a specific purpose, such as flag raising songs, grand entry songs, and honor songs. They are sung in their original American Indian language and are considered one way old traditions are orally handed down to new generations.

All of the various dance categories have corresponding songs with different drum beats and different paces, some fast, some slow, some changing pace within a given song. The combination of drumming and singing can be extremely efficacious, stimulating the dancers, making their hearts beat faster, and even exciting spectators, for example, to feel as if their hair is standing on end or as if they are unable to keep their feet from moving. Occasionally, as a result of the music, crowds of spectators can not remain seated and rise to stand and dance in place in their response to the music.

Some drum songs are not accompanied by lyrics or vocal sounds of any kind, but merely provide a rhythmic base for the dancing. And some songs are accompanied by "vocables" or chants that are not lyrics, but rhythmically correspond with the drum beats. They are not random utterances, though. They may or may not have specific meaning and are a learned and practiced series of utterances. Sometimes a single chanter, or maybe several chanters, chant together, all making the same sounds, none of which are words in any language.

The Grand Entry

THERE ARE THREE GRAND ENTRIES (*see* Color Section the Grand Entry) at the Mankato Powwow. They are scheduled to begin at 1:00 p.m. on Saturday, 7:00 p.m. Saturday, and at 1:00 p.m. on Sunday. Each one of the grand entries is a great spectacle, a grand parade, a fine photo opportunity, and a very moving experience for all the dancers and all the spectators. Hundreds of dancers appear in each of these events, all of them dressed in their finest beaded buckskins and varied feathered regalia. They line up at the east gate of the arena and, on a signal, when the host drum begins to beat, the dancers begin to dance into the arena and dance around the arena in a clockwise direction. The flag bearers enter first, according to tradition, followed by the veterans. The eagle-feathered staffs representing various tribes, communities, or families are followed by flag bearers carrying the flags of the United States, Canada, and a Prisoner of War flag. Next in the line are the princesses, representing many different American Indian communities, followed by the adult male dancers, who come from many different tribes wearing varieties of regalia. All the dancers are resplendent in beaded buckskins, feathered head dresses, feathered bustles, shields, and other accoutrements. They are followed by the adult women traditional dancers, who in turn are followed by the jingle dress dancers and then the fancy shawl dancers and many children dancing in regalia, the boys coming ahead of the girls. All of the participant dancers in the grand entry must be wearing dancing regalia and must be registered as dancers.

At the start of the grand entry, the emcee directs the spectators to stand and remove their hats or head gear out of respect for the flags and the ceremony. Spectators are asked to remain standing until the grand entry ceremony is completed. The emcee will introduce the flags and the flag bearers, veterans group and any dignitaries participating in the grand entry. The flags are set into place at the center of the arena and a prayer song and a flag song then end the ceremony.

During the powwow, many different kinds of dances take place. At some powwows the dancing is a contest, and the best dancers are awarded prizes. The dancing at the Mankato Powwow in not a contest, but the dancers are still identified by a number that they receive at registration. They fasten the number to their dance regalia. With the help of that number, the dancers can be monitored to record the extent to which each dancer participates in the dancing. This, in turn, helps powwow officials in fairly dispensing the money obtained from donations and other sources. For many, these payments to the dancers amount to little more than gas money to cover travel expenses from distant places, but without that little bit of help, some of the dancers would not be able to make the trip to the powwow. Many of them come from very poor communities.

Grass Dances

Several sources of information give different information about the origin of the grass dance, one of the oldest of dances. One version of its origin, easily found in several sources on the Internet, is that when a scouting party was looking for a new location for a gathering of any kind, upon finding it they would dance around, flattening the grass to prepare the area. The prairies were covered with long grass in the old days. Sometimes the grass was more than three feet tall. The movements the dancers made when flattening the grass were incorporated into the dance and are repeated in the dancing today.

Another version of the origin of the grass dance[3] relates that when a hunting party would leave camp in the winter, they would take with them a supply of long grass fixed under their belts for use in starting a fire or for stuffing into their moccasins to keep their feet warm. This version of the origin is offered as explanation of why the regalia of grass dancers typically includes long strands of cloth or other material to simulate long grass. (See Color Plate of Grass Dance regalia)

Men's Traditional Dance

The men's traditional dance is a hold over from times when war parties or hunting parties returned to their village and had a dance to celebrate their battles or the successes of their hunt. In their dance, the men would dance in a manner that would reflect their exploits, tell the story of the pursuit of their enemy or prey. Their dancing regalia is often decorated with bead work or quill work but the colors of their regalia are more subdued than in other dance regalia. On their backside, traditional dancers wear one or two circular bustles of eagle feathers representing the circular unity of everything. The eagle feathers spike on the bustle pointing upward, representing a channel between the Great Spirit and all things on Earth.

Traditional dancers are often veterans who, as they dance, carry items that symbolize their status as warriors, such as shields, weapons, an honor staff, or a medicine wheel. An interesting and ironic note in this regard is the fact that Amos Crooks (*see* Color Plate Six) had his own Seventh Cavalry patch on his shield. He served in the Army for fifteen years and did three tours of duty in Korea during the Korean War. What makes that ironic is the fact that the Seventh Cavalry was General Custer's outfit at the Battle of the Little Big Horn. An honor staff is decorated with eagle feathers to represent accomplishments in battle and to challenge the enemy. A medicine wheel may be carried as a reminder of the wisdom of the four directions, unity, and the cycle of all things in the universe.

The traditional dance step in done with the ball of the foot just touching the ground on one drum beat and the whole of the same foot landing on the ground on the next drum beat. Then that same step is repeated with the other foot. The dancer's movements may be original according to his own story being told, but the movements are usually patterned after animals or birds, and may be an imitation of tracking or an imitation of an animal itself. The dancing is often performed in a crouched posture. (See Color Plate of Traditional Dance regalia)

Women's Traditional Dance

TRADITIONALLY, WOMEN DANCED only to certain songs or on special occasions. Even then their dancing was restrained in its movements. Women stayed mostly in the background at dances. When they did dance, the dancing consisted of standing almost stationary while bending the knees slightly to produce a minimal up and down movement of the body. At the same time the feet shifted slightly to move the dancer forward with small steps. There is no twirling or high stepping. There may be slight turns that some say simulate the way women looked for their warriors to come home.

In the mid-1800s when beads were acquired through trade, the style for the women's traditional dance outfit was to bead the entire top of the dress. The design of each dress had a symbolic meaning to the individual owner. The dresses were decorated with ribbons, elk's teeth, and shells, among other things, and knee-high leggings, beaded or concho belts, and various kinds of jewelry (hair ties, earrings, chokers, and necklaces) were worn. Most traditional dancers wear or carry a shawl, and some carry an eagle or hawk feather fan or a single feather. (*See* Color Plate of Women's Traditional Dancers) At certain points in a dance, women may hear words that are meaningful to them. They may signal their pride and acknowledge the words by raising their fans. Others raise their fans during the honor beats of a song.

Fancy Dance

W HEN DANCING, A FANCY DANCER is often like a whirlwind. Fancy dancers wear more regalia than other dancers, and the regalia is more frilly, more feathery. The dancer is almost surrounded by it. Sometimes during the dance the dancer cannot be seen at all, becoming just a blur of regalia whirling around like a tornado. Fancy dancers are mostly boys and young men because this style of dancing requires more agility and stamina than most of the older guys can muster. This is a relatively new addition to the dances, originating in Oklahoma in the early 1900s. The fancy dance is based on the standard "double step" of the traditional and grass dances, but goes beyond that to include elaborate movements, increased speed, acrobatic steps and body motions, and a lot of whirling and spinning. The fancy dance is also a free-style dance so there is much variation from one dancer to another. However, they too must follow the beat of the drum and stop with both feet on the ground when the music stops. (*See* Color Plate of Fancy Dancers)

Jingle Dress Dance

T HE JINGLE DRESS DANCE EVOLVED from a holy man's dream. In his dream, four women wearing jingle dresses appeared before him. They showed him how to make the dresses, what types of songs went with them, and how the dance was performed. The dress was made of cloth with hundreds of metal cones or jingles covering it. The dance movements were very lively and made the jingles swing and contact each other to make a jingling sound. The jingling of the dresses made a sound he found very enjoyable.

Upon awakening, he and his wife made four jingle dresses, called the four young women who, in his dream, had worn them, and had them put on the dresses. They all went to the dance where he told of his dream, and the women danced. They had to keep time with the drumming and to stop dancing with both feet on the ground at the last beat of the drum. Jingle dancers are a younger group than the traditional women dancers, probably because of the vigorous dancing required.

In the late 1920s, the jingle dress dance was given to the Dakota by the Ojibwe. It then spread westward into the Dakotas and Montana. Interestingly the jingles of a jingle dress were made out of the metal lids of Copenhagen snuff cans. Some claim that a real jingle dress is made with 365 jingles on it and, traditionally, a prayer would be said as each jingle is sewn into the dress. The round lid of the snuff can was rolled up to have a conical shape and then attached to the dress so it would swing. Even today when jingles are manufactured for the making of jingle dresses, they are often knock offs of the original Copenhagen can lid. (*See* Color Plate of Jingle Dress Dancers)

Fancy Shawl Dance

THE WOMEN'S FANCY DANCE or shawl dance is a relatively new addition to powwow dances in the same way that the men's fancy dance is. In fact, this dance is also called the "women's fancy dance." Until recently, women performed their fancy dancing in traditional regalia. In the 1930s and 1940s, young women would show off the shawls they made by doing some fancy footwork at the dances. Some say that's how the women's fancy shawl dance was born. In the 1990s shawls replaced the blankets and buffalo robes young girls traditionally wore in public.

The fancy shawl dance regalia are comprised of a decorated knee-length cloth dress, beaded moccasins with matching leggings, a fancy shawl, and various pieces of jewelry. (*See* Color Plate of Fancy Shawl Dancers) The dance itself is very similar to the men's fancy dance with a lot of twirling. The trend is moving toward even more active dancing, especially spinning. Footwork and the use of the shawl are the main components of the dance. As in other dances, the fancy shawl dancer must stay in sync with the beat of the drum and stop with both feet on the ground at the last drum beat.

Intertribal Dance

EVERYONE IS WELCOME TO DANCE in an intertribal dance, even the spectators. People of all kinds and any age are welcome to enter the arena and dance. It is not as much a particular type of dance as it is a chance for everyone to dance. The dance movement is in a clockwise direction around the dance arena. The wearing of dance regalia is not required. Ordinary street clothes will do. The basic step is the same as for traditional dances: the ball of the foot is tapped on the ground on one beat and placed flatly on the ground with the next beat, and this action is then repeated with the opposite foot. However, if that proves to be too difficult, simply walking or shuffling around to the beat of the drum is perfectly acceptable. The main focus of this dance is to get everyone to participate and mingle.

* * *

THE FOREGOING DANCES ARE COMMONLY SEEN at the Mankato Powwow, but they do not comprise an exhaustive list. The ancient culture of the Dakota included many dances not often seen these days for obvious reasons. These included buffalo dances, fire dances, war dances, victory dances, and scalp dances.[4] In the old days the Dakota often battled with the Ojibwe or others, and they would have a war dance before sending a war party into harm's way, and a victory dance when the battle was over if it was successful. But the Dakota are not at war with anyone anymore so war dances and victory dances are not seen at the powwow. And since the buffalo were killed by white men nearly to extinction, buffalo hunting and buffalo dances came to an end also.

* * *

ON ONE OCCASION A FEMALE ACQUAINTANCE came to my camp at the Mankato Powwow to visit and to tell me that she had only recently discovered that there were American Indians in her family tree. To celebrate her new-found American Indian roots she came from Minneapolis to Mankato to attend the powwow. She was a well-educated and quite attractive young lady who was married to a professional colleague of mine. I congratulated her on her discovery and told her she should be very proud. That wasn't necessary because she was already more than sufficiently proud. She was quite excited about it. But it developed that she needed a little more education about American Indian dancing.

Some time later, the arena director came to my camp to talk to me about her. He told me that he had to remove her from the arena in the middle of a dance because her regalia and the way she was dancing were not at all traditional. Removing someone like that from a dance, especially during a dance, was an extremely unusual thing to happen. I learned that she had dressed in her own version of dance regalia, which truly was anything but traditional. Instead, she wore a buckskin shirt and a short, above-the-knees buckskin skirt with fringes on both. Most likely, she had made this outfit herself. That was as close to traditional as it came, although she also wore beaded moccasins that she likely purchased, perhaps even at the powwow. Joining in a dance, she had her own version of dancing too, which consisted of some rhythmic twirling, high stepping, high kicking, and many seductive bumps and grinds. She drew a lot of attention from everyone, spectators, dancers, and powwow officials. She was known to be somewhat exhibitionistic to begin with, and she likely was not bothered at all by the attention she received from everyone. Quite to the contrary, she probably enjoyed it. Being removed from the arena was less likely to have embarrassed her than to have given her an acute attack of indignation and puzzlement. I think she then left the powwow in a huff and went home. I didn't see her again, but I would have liked to talk with her to encourage her to learn about dancing and regalia. To my knowledge she never did come back to another Mankato Powwow, which is quite sad.

Notes

1. Pond. p.81.
2. Pond.
3. Oneroad and Skinner, p.79.
4. Oneroad and Skinner.

Chapter Eight

Ceremonies at the Powwow

The Ceremonial Blessing of the Sacred Arena

THE DAY BEFORE THE POWWOW is to begin, the dance arena (the circle for the dance) is laid out with a diameter of 165 feet. In the center of the circle are flag poles for the American flag, the Canadian flag, and the flag for Prisoners of War. Benches are placed around the perimeter of the circle for dancers to use between dances. Outside the benches is another circle comprised of bleachers for spectators. At recent powwows the fourteen bleachers have been absolutely full of spectators with hundreds more finding standing room around them. In addition, many spectators bring their own lawn chairs, especially if they are elderly. Lawn chairs pack the area between the bleachers and the benches around the arena.

On Friday morning, the first day of the powwow, the arena is blessed by the spiritual leader of the powwow in a sunrise ceremony. He prays with his pipe to the Great Spirit (Wakan Tonka), to Mother Earth, and to the four directions for the blessing of the arena. Then the flags are raised and from that time until the end of the powwow the dance arena is considered a sacred place, like a church. Rules of etiquette that would apply in a church should be observed in the arena.

No playing or buffoonery is allowed in the arena. Pets are to be kept out of it. Alcohol and drugs are prohibited not only in the arena but throughout the entire powwow area. Anyone found to be using them is asked to leave, and, if resistant, they are made to leave.

Many spiritual ceremonies take place in the circle during the powwow. The powwow is not just a *wacipi* or dance, although the drumming and dancing continue much of the time. Songs, drumming and dancing are a part of almost every ceremony. Some sacred Indian ceremonies are strictly private and not seen by the general public. Examples of these are the sun dance ceremonies and fleshing ceremonies.

I have heard that a fleshing ceremony was held privately in connection with the December 26th Memorial Run. At this ceremony thirty-eight small pieces of skin were removed from the upper arms of a respected elder to honor the thirty-eight warriors hanged. However, a large number of ceremonies take place and are witnessed by the public in the sacred circle over the powwow weekend.

Naming Ceremonies

MANY YEARS AGO, THE ANCIENT DAKOTA custom was to name children according to the order of their birth. A first-born boy would be called "Chaska" and a first born girl would be "Winona." There were names for boys and girls up to the fifth of each born. Sometimes these ordinal names are applied through the child's life, but not necessarily. If the child became specially talented in one way or another, or achieved something special, a new name could be acquired and the ordinal name abandoned. The change of names often occurred at a dance or ceremony of one kind or another, to make the change publically known and to credit or honor the individual properly with the special talent, achievement, or deed.[1]

Naming ceremonies were common at powwows in the past, but today this kind of ceremony usually takes place in the privacy of the home. If it happens at the powwow, as it sometimes does, it would likely occur in the morning when the number of spectators is relatively small. In this ceremony an individual is given a name, usually a new name in the language. The name and the ceremony are conferred upon the individual by an interested person or group, and the event and the name often reflect the reason for which it is given. For example, a hypothetical one, a young military veteran returning from war after having been decorated for bravery in combat might be given a name to honor him publically at a powwow for what he did. His new honor name could be something like "Fights with No Fear." This name would be given in the Dakota language, in which case it would be something like "Kokita sne." The soldier would also traditionally participate in a sun dance (non-public) where a spiritual ceremony would take place to relieve him of any negative residuals or consequences of his heroism.

Mike Ballard, a former president of the Mdewakanton Club, was given his Indian name, Tate Ob Mani, (Walks with the Wind), at the Mankato Powwow. Amos Owen gave him this name to honor him because he was the vendor coordinator at the powwow at the time and he was "here and there and everywhere" as he busily went about in his duties.

Honor Ceremonies

OTHER KINDS OF HONOR CEREMONIES take place at the powwow to show gratitude and respect to an individual for any kind of outstanding quality, accomplishment, or service done. The individual being honored is called forth to receive the honor. Usually, a prepared citation is read aloud for everyone to hear. The person being honored is given a blanket or a plaque or some other symbol of the honor ceremony. Then everyone lines up to pass by the honoree, shake the individual's hand and extend congratulations, and enter into the honor dance that follows. Dancing regalia is not required to participate in an honor dance. As mentioned previously, Bill Bassett, the one-time Mankato city manager, was honored in this manner for his help in getting the powwow established in Mankato. Several people or a group of people could be honored at the same time during an honor ceremony.

Miss Mahkato and Junior Miss Mahkato

ANNUALLY, A NEW "MISS MAHKATO" is selected from the dancers based in part on the performance of the girl's dancing at the powwow, but also based on the known accomplishments of the girl. A group of elder women judges make the selection. Usually these women have known all the contestants since they were born.

Art Owen addressing Powwow Committee members being honored. (Author's private collection)

A "Junior Miss Mahkato" is similarly selected, and both girls are awarded the title of "Princess," as well as a beaded crown and a sash, which they will wear as they represent the Mankato Powwow at other powwows throughout the next year. (*See* color plate of Princess)

Wedding Ceremonies

WEDDINGS ARE NOT SO COMMON AT POWWOWS anymore, but they took place there regularly years ago, and they still happen occasionally. But even if weddings don't happen at the powwow often, the ground work for weddings still takes place there. Powwows are events where people from distant places meet one another, paving the way for relationships to develop. Two very prominent people in the Mde-wakanton Club, Bruce and Sheryl Dowlin, were married in an Indian ceremony in 1986 after they met in activities associated with the powwow. The formation of new relationships between young people was a much more important function of the powwow in the past, when it was critical for young boys and girls in one tribe to meet others from a different tribe, but today this function isn't important.

Today, the world has become a smaller place than it was many years ago. Travel is easier. Not only do many young people have cars and cell phones, but they also have access to the Internet. Meeting people is no longer a problem.

Give-aways

DAKOTA TRADITION HOLDS that the richest person in a given tribe is not the man who has the most horses or wives or who owns the most property, but is the one who, when compared with others, has given more of his belongings to others. Such a person will have a high status in his or her community even though no longer in possession of much materially.

A "Give Away" is a ceremony to celebrate anything worth celebrating or honoring. It could be celebration of a healing, a birth, a birthday, graduation from school, or any other kind of accomplishment. The remarkable thing about this old custom within the American Indian culture is that the honoree is the one who is the giver of gifts. That is the opposite of what non-American Indian cultures do as a rule. In those cultures, the "birthday boy" gets the gifts instead of being the giver of gifts to the guests.

Condolences

WHEN SOMEONE HAS PASSED AWAY, the Dakota grieving customs are quite complicated and some of them are severe. Grieving is expected to last for four years. As part of this process, a dance might be sponsored to help those who are in mourning or to remember whomever it was who died.

Adoption

AN ADOPTION CEREMONY TAKES PLACE when someone is taken in as a member of a family or tribe. The ceremony is usually accompanied by a dance.

Bullet Proofing

I HAVE MET TWO VIETNAM WAR VETERANS at the powwow who believe they owe their lives to the bullet proofing ceremonies held for them before they went to war. These ceremonies include dancing and singing to honor the soldier going to war and prayers to the Great Spirit (Wakan Tonka) asking for protection for the soldier in combat.

Healing

MEDICINE MEN AND DAKOTA SPIRITUAL LEADERS invoke the powers of the Great Spirit to make sick people well. They actually do more than that, but in this context, that's what they do. When someone in the community is sick, a ceremony at the powwow might be held to pray for the recovery of the person. Such a ceremony would be conducted by a spiritual leader. This ceremony would likely include prayers, probably a song, and drumming and dancing. The healing process might also involve the use of a variety of herbs, potions, and prayers administered by a medicine man.

There is some confusion regarding the use of the term "medicine man." To American Indians, a medicine man is like a doctor, using herbs, potions, and anything else that works to heal wounds, fix injuries or make sick people well. Sometimes a spiritual leader is called a medicine man, especially when he uses prayer to invoke the help of the Great Mystery to aid in the recovery of someone who is ill or injured. People sometimes call that activity "making medicine." Therein lies the confusion. Small wonder that the two are confused, but there is a difference.

It appears also that a "healer" might be neither a recognized medicine man nor a spiritual leader of any sort. A healer is more like a touch therapist but also might use prayers in his ministrations, invoking the help of the Great Mystery and/or the spirits of great chiefs long passed. In his book, *Mystic Warriors of the Plains*, Thomas Mails described it this way:

> The holy men and doctors, while lacking in great degree the educated skills of modern priests, psychologists, and modern doctors, did indeed work amazing cures from time to time because they learned to apply herbs and to manage the psychology of bringing a patient's faith and will to live to the fore. Above all, the holy men and doctors understood themselves to be tubes through which the One-Above worked. Once they had properly purified themselves, He reached down through them to touch the patient and to accomplish the actual healing.[2]

Some additional clarification of these terms can be found in authoritative sources such as Black Elk's book, *The Sacred Pipe*, edited and recorded by Joseph Eppes Brown.[3]

The House Call

JOHN FIRE LAME DEER, a medicine man, told the following story to Bud Lawrence when Bud met him at "Indian Week," a special event at Mankato State College. Lame Deer said he was driving through the Mesquakie Indian Reservation in Iowa when he had a very strange experience. He had never visited this reservation before and was totally unfamiliar with the area and didn't know anyone who lived there. But as he passed by a certain house he had a compelling urge to stop and go to the house. He felt as if he were being called to the house and that someone in the house needed his help.

He knocked on the door to the house and a man responded.

"I know that you don't know me, but I am a medicine man and I want to know if there is someone here who needs my help."

"Yes," said Harvey Davenport, the man who answered the door. "My wife in very ill and I'm glad you're here."

"I'll be right back," said the medicine man as he went to his car to get his bag of medicines.

He returned immediately, and Harvey showed him in and led him to the bedroom where his wife was lying in bed with a high fever.

Through much of the night John Fire Lame Deer prayed and chanted in the Dakota language. He also administered some potions. And in the morning, Harvey's wife was feeling much better, and John Fire Lame Deer went on his way after a good breakfast and a short rest.

When the medicine man told Bud Lawrence this story, it stuck in Bud's mind. He could hardly believe it. After all, what was the likelihood that, without being called to do anything, a medicine man would stop at an unfamiliar house and find somebody sick there? It was a bit incredible. Bud knew Harvey Davenport very well. Six months after hearing Lame Deer's story, at the next Mankato Powwow, Bud asked Harvey if he had ever had an experience with a medicine man, carefully avoiding any promp that he was talking about Lame Deer and carefully avoiding any mention of the story he had heard from Lame Deer.

To Bud's amazement, Harvey responded, "Oh, sure. A medicine man came to my house one time . . ." and Harvey retold the same story from his own point of view, confirming all details of what Lame Deer had told Bud.

* * *

At the powwow, one might encounter an individual identified as a "healer." Tom Quick Bear is one. He is like what is more commonly known as a "faith healer" or "touch healer." He is not exactly a medicine man or spiritual leader, but if asked to help with a pain or an ailment of any kind he might wave his hands around one's body and put his hands on the person, all the while praying to the Great Spirit and invoking the spirits of great chiefs, like Sitting Bull and Crazy Horse to come to the person's aid to help overcome pain or ailment, or whatever the problem is. Many people do appear to get some immediate relief from their pains or problems with this kind of treatment. But even many American Indians are skeptical and distrustful of these "healers." Even some of those with a strong belief in American Indian spirituality apparently think that the benefits of this kind of treatment are nothing more than a placebo effect. Still, even some accredited hospitals employ methods like "touch therapy" that closely resemble Tom Quick Bear's treatments. St Mary's Hospital in Rochester, Minnesota, is respected world wide for its medical care and is known to employ touch therapy occasionally. People often do get some relief from these methods. To the extent that they actually do help people they are recognized as useful, even in scientific circles.

Rain Ceremonies

THE WEATHER IS NOT ALWAYS COOPERATIVE during the powwow, although the sun would usually be shining. In the third week of September in Minnesota the weather is usually quite nice during the day, cool at night (perfect campfire weather), but the weather can be variable. There have been several instances of heavy rain, which were inconvenient for the powwow. Gate money would be diminished because few spectators would venture out in the rain. But the rain was especially disastrous for the dancers. Heavy rain would be a serious setback for the dancers wearing moccasins and dressed in beaded buckskins and adorned with a multitude of feathers. Everything out in the open could get soaked. Electrical equipment could be damaged or destroyed. The drums would be ruined. The hundreds of dancers could turn the arena into mud. Still, if it were raining at the time of a grand entry ceremony, the dancing likely would proceed nevertheless.

On one such occasion, following a dance in which everyone got soaked, Amos Owen commented, "The spirits are weeping." The American Indians decided to have a ceremony to stop the rain and the emcee called for a fire to be placed in the middle of the arena. As the head of the grounds crew at the time, it was my responsibility to make the fire. There was little dry wood available. I had a good fire going at my camp, however, as always from some days before the beginning of the powwow to the end of the powwow. I recruited some club members to help me move my fire to the arena. We loaded the burning wood and large pieces of coals onto a metal grate and carried the fire to the middle of the arena and dumped it on the wet ground. But transporting had nearly extinguished the fire, and there were no more flames. Putting it on the wet ground didn't help it much either. So I got on my knees and proceeded to pile the embers and blow on them in an attempt to get the fire going.

Then I heard a loud and stern voice on the loud speaker saying, "Stop blowing on that fire like that!"

I looked up, somewhat startled. I saw Porky White at the microphone in the bandstand. "You're not supposed to blow on that fire like that!" he said.

His tone sounded a bit angry, as if I were being scolded. With a couple of hundred people looking at me, I was embarrassed. This was to be a sacred fire. I didn't know that blowing on a sacred fire was taboo. I backed away completely, wondering whether the fire would actually start to burn because the soaking rain was still coming down on it. But suddenly the fire started burning brightly, with flames rising surprisingly high despite the rain. Someone brought dry kindling and a couple of dry logs to lay on the fire, and the fire was well established. Some Dakota prayers were said around it, and, after a while, the rain gradually stopped falling and the sun emerged from the clouds. The dancing resumed and for the remaining part of the weekend the weather was sunny. But on Monday morning, when all the dancers and concessionaires were gone and the volunteers and Mdewakanton Club members were cleaning up the park, it was raining again.

Such mysterious happenings make one ponder. It was fascinating to me how that fire perked up even in the rain. And was it really just a coincidence that the rain actually stopped after that ceremony? And was it a coincidence that the weather stayed nice for the next day and a half? The weather report hadn't indicated this would happen. I'm now inclined to believe that the Dakota prayers had something to do with it.

Of course, there are rain dances for the purpose of bringing *on* the rain when the weather is too dry and a drought is threatening farming efforts. These dances will not be seen at the powwow, however, for obvious reasons. The powwow is much more successful in good weather.

Remembrances (Meals)

THE MDEWAKANTON ASSOCIATION provides several meals for the campers, dancers, drum groups, and volunteers at the powwow, at noon on both Saturday and Sunday, and the evening meal on Saturday. Those three meals are usually catered by a supplier from Mankato, but sometimes the meals are prepared right at the powwow where they are served. The meals are complete with a salad, meat, fruit, vegetables, bread, dessert, and a choice of beverages. As many as a thousand people come to eat at the cook shack every time a meal is served.

Often one or more of the big meals will be sponsored by a donor in remembrance of a departed family member or to honor somebody. These can be catered or prepared at the cook shack by the people who sponsor it. In that case, in addition to the standard fare, there might be something special offered, some traditional Indian food such as corn chowder, or tripe soup, or a wild berry pudding (*wojapi*), or perhaps a favorite food of the person being remembered or honored. The volunteers at the cook shack are always supervised by an American Indian woman. In 2011 this was Leslie Walking Elk who was also a women's traditional dancer. Sadly, she passed away only weeks following the powwow (*see* Color Plate of Leslie Elk).

The evening meal on Sunday was different because the powwow would be ending and many of the people at the powwow were packing up and getting ready

Meals at the cook shack are served by volunteers. (Author's private collection)

for the trip home. The association would pack bag lunches for them to eat on their way home. The lunches would consist of a sandwich, potato chips, and some fruit. Canned or bottled soft drinks or milk might also be available to them. Nobody would go away hungry.

For many years, a complementary breakfast was also served at the cook shack. Bud Lawrence would arrange for Hardee's Restaurant to provide biscuits and gravy and coffee for all comers. This happened for many years until breakfast was served by a member of the Mdewakanton Association as a remembrance for her mother.

Eva Klein served a free and nourishing breakfast to all comers at the powwow every Friday, Saturday, and Sunday morning for twenty years. At her own expense, she served bacon and eggs, fried potatoes, rolls and donuts, oatmeal, bread, coffee, and juice or milk to hundreds who took advantage of her generous hospitality. She started out small, inviting friends and whoever might be passing by her camp to join her in the breakfast meal. But it was a very good meal and the word got around fast. Soon there were hundreds of campers lining up to eat. She fed them all. The menu changed slightly after about ten years as a matter of convenience. The last year that bacon was served as part of the breakfast they actually served 169 pounds of it. Most of it had to be fried up in advance of the breakfast and frying that much bacon was about three and one-half hours of work even though Eva's husband, Dave, had made a giant frying pan about two feet in diameter. It was a lot easier and more practical to serve ham instead of bacon, so the switch was made. The big frying pan continued to be used for making the best fried potatoes anyone had ever eaten. To put an approximate quantity on the amount of food served at breakfast in recent years, according to Eva, she and her volunteers served (in the three day weekend) about 1,800 eggs, fifty pounds of ham, and 225 pounds of fried potatoes, all at no cost to the consumers. Because of the size to which this event grew, the Mdewakanton Association finally did pitch in to cover some of the costs in recent years, and occasionally campers would drop off a couple of dozen eggs or some bacon at Eva'a camp, but in large part the breakfast meal was still Eva's contribution to the powwow in honor of her mother. To top that off, though it needed no topping, she also provided a complete late-night meal to all those who attended the sweat ceremony.

Eva did this to honor her mother, Clara Aubin, an Ojibwe Indian who had passed away in February 1990. Clara had loved to attend the powwow since the very beginning. Eva's father, Ray Aubin, was once enrolled at the White Earth Indian Reservation and was one of the signers of the Articles of Incorporation when the Mdewakanton Club was first organized. Because of the involvement of her parents with the powwow, Eva has been attending since she was a young woman and has been a very devoted and active member of the Mdewakanton Club for many years. Eva is enrolled as a member of the Minnesota Chippewa Tribe at White Earth, Minnesota.

Notes

1. Oneroad and Skinner, p.88-89.
2. Mails, p. 584.
3. p. 45.

Thirty-five to forty-five vendor sites circle the bleachers and spectators. (Author's private collection)

Chapter Nine

Vendors

Varieties of Merchandise

AT THE PERIPHERY OF THE POWWOW area is a circle of thirty to forty vendors. These travel from one powwow to another selling their wares all summer long. Several of the vendors at the powwow hawk American Indian jewelry, including bracelets, necklaces, rings, watches, pendants, broaches, and such things as fountain pens and belt buckles adorned with jewels. The "jewels" are usually turquoise, obsidian, or other kinds of semi-precious stones. Some of the items for sale are quite expensive, others very reasonable. The vendors generally stand behind their goods and are quite open and honest about the quality, but if the Mdewakanton Association's vendor coordinator learns of someone dishonest, that vendor might not be invited to return to the Mankato Powwow.

Many vendors sell Indian blankets, shawls, moccasins, boots, and other Indian clothing of all kinds. This is very popular merchandise at the powwow, and it is usually of good quality and fairly priced. These make good souvenirs of the powwow. Officials try to make sure the merchandise is genuine. Foreign-made knockoffs are discouraged.

American Indian artwork is plentiful at the powwow—paintings, sculpture, and pottery. Many of the quilts and blankets made by the American Indians are works of art, and vendors selling them might be the American Indian artist who made them. Trade beads, leather, game skins, furs, tanned hides, and other materials for making Indian art are also available at the powwow. As one strolls by the concessions, it is common to see vendors engaged in making the objects being sold.

American Indian "artifacts" are also popular as souvenirs. These include dream catchers, rattles, turtle shells, pipes, mandellas, leather pouches, and perhaps even bows and arrows and lances. A dream catcher is a wooden hoop laced with a web inside and may be adorned with feathers or other adornments suspended from the bottom. It is hung above a bed or in a window of the bedroom. According to legend, the web has a hole in the middle of it that allows bad dreams and spirits to pass through and leave your home. The catcher prevents good dreams and spirits from leaving so they remain a part of your life. Sacred American Indian objects (such as buffalo skulls and blessed peace pipes) are not permitted to be displayed or sold.

Food Vendors

AMERICAN INDIAN FOOD DOES NOT GET much recognition for being fine cuisine or as good recipes for sensitive tastes. American Indians of days gone by were not noted as having a delicate palate. Rather, Indian food of old was much more likely to be characterized as survival food. American Indians were hunter/gatherers—they lived off the land. When times were good and the buffalo was plentiful, they feasted on buffalo steaks and meaty buffalo stews. For variety they might have roasted prairie chickens or antelope, deer, fish, rabbits, and ducks or other small game. When food was plentiful, they had ways of preserving food to make it available for harder times. They dried meat in the sun or smoked it over fires. Campfires had meat hanging over them being preserved more often than not. Buffalo jerky was flavorful and nutritious, did not spoil quickly and remained edible for months. Grains and berries and edible roots were also gathered and dried. These foods would usually sustain them over the occasional long and lean periods when absolutely no game could be found.

But when game was not available and they had used up their preserves, they still had to eat. So, they ate what was available to stay alive. Sometimes what they ate were things most of us would not find appetizing—prairie dogs, muskrats, snakes, lizards, and even worms might appear on the menu. In the hardest of times, even their own dogs would go into the soup. Today, they joke about it. When a dog ran through the arena at a recent Mankato Powwow, the emcee, Jerry Dearly, announced over the public address system that "Somebody had better get that dog out of the arena or he'll end up in tonight's soup!" But at the Mankato Powwow no "desperation foods" are found at the food concessions.

Traditional American Indian food does not have much seasoning, but some of it is very flavorful nevertheless. They did not, as a rule, use salt or pepper because these were not available to them. They did season with the seeds and leaves of many plants available. Sage leaves, dried and crushed, were a common ingredient in their soups and stews. Wild honey and maple syrup were what they used as sweeteners.

At the Mankato Powwow the coordinators of the vendors have tried to keep the food vendors' offerings in line with what the American Indians traditionally might have eaten. There are usually eight to ten food concessions at the powwow. A greater number of applications to sell food items at the powwow are received, but the number accepted is limited to eight or ten. The vendor coordinator gives preference to American Indians selling American Indian foods. Such foods as wild rice, hot soups, fry bread, buffalo burgers, and corn are encouraged. Sugared mini-donuts, spaghetti, and Chinese foods are deemed not appropriate at a traditional powwow and are discouraged. But to limit the food offerings to traditional Indian food is not possible. The vendors are given a lot of latitude in their offerings. The acceptability of shaved ice was discussed at length and finally was allowed because during the cold season American Indians ate shaved ice flavored with maple syrup. They ate game animals, so meats of a variety are considered traditional. They also made flour from some of the grains they gathered, and then they made bread dough and fried it in animal fat. Indian fry bread is a very popular food at the powwow. Corn is also a well-known Indian food. They ate corn long before the white man got it from them. But the Mankato Powwow is held in late September so the sweet corn season is usually over by that time. At one recent powwow a farmer who had a late crop of sweet corn sold corn on the cob as the only food at his concession and he sold out completely in no time at all.

The "Gate"

THE "GATE" IS THE MDEWAKANTON ASSOCIATION'S own concession, at which all visitors to the powwow are requested to make a one-time five-dollar donation to the general powwow fund when they enter the grounds. Those who don't are still admitted and welcomed. Everyone who donates is given a button souvenir of the powwow and a program of scheduled events. Nobody is turned away unless they are obviously intoxicated. The use of alcohol or drugs is strictly prohibited at the powwow.

Between mid-morning and mid-evening, members of the Mdewakanton Club stop all the traffic entering the powwow grounds to welcome the visitors and ask for the donation. Even members of the club and vendors are asked to make a donation. Almost everyone makes the five dollar donation. The money obtained in this way is a very important part of the funding for the powwow.

Chapter Ten

The Spectators

AT POWWOWS OLD ACQUAINTANCES are often renewed. One never knows who will be there. All kinds of people come to the powwow, some just to see the dancing and the splendid and varied regalia. The Mdewakanton Association's current website reports that nearly 70,000 people have visited the powwow since June 2001. Some camp for the weekend and enjoy the powwow from beginning to end. Some old timers are always there, year after year. Former Mdewakanton Club members still come to the powwow, enjoying seeing old friends there. Many spectators come to enjoy the powwow for the first time. Some use the powwow as a family reunion just like the American Indians did in the old days.

One couple, Dianne and John Shoemaker, come every year. They have attended every Mankato Powwow since the very beginning, and John proudly wears all the powwow buttons he has collected over the years, all thirty-six of them. (*See* Color Plate of the Schoemakers) The 2010 Powwow is the thirty-eighth, but there are only thirty-six buttons because tickets were used at the first two powwows instead of buttons, but John still has the tickets from the first two powwows, carefully preserved.

In recent decades, three or four thousand spectators visit the powwow over the weekend. Most of them are locals, curious to see American Indians dancing. Some spectators, however, have come from as far as the other side of the world, having heard about the Mankato Powwow and wanting to learn more about it. One spectator was an American Indian boy who rode his painted pony all the way from Nebraska to attend.

Admission to the powwow is free. The donations received at the gate are used to help support the dancers who often travel many hundreds of miles at their own expense to attend. Many Indian communities are very poor. Many of the dancers who come from these impoverished communities use the dance money for gas and to defray at least some of the cost of their travel. They appreciate the provided meals.

Campers

ONE OF THE MAJOR CONTRIBUTIONS Mankato makes to the powwow is free use of the Land of Memories Park. They let campers into the park free for several days at that time. The park fills with campers, but not just because it's free. Camping at the powwow is a very special experience, much more than ordinary camping. During the evenings of the powwow the air is filled with a pleasant, smoky smell of campfires and the aroma of a variety of exotic foods being cooked on them. Although there are always many food concessions around the dance arena and some free meals are served to campers at the cook shack, many campers like to cook some things for themselves—hotdogs or smores or stew as they relax around their fires and exchange stories when the dancing is done. (*See* Color Plate of Author's camp, 2005)

Sometimes the evenings in mid-September are quite cool and the campfires provide warmth, but they are just as important for their pleasant ambiance. Campers show up with every kind of gear imaginable—expensive recreational vehicles to tents to sleeping bags under the stars. Kenny Ray once came with a huge horse trailer converted into a camper.

At least one guy came to the powwow without any kind of camping equipment but he camped anyway. Late one evening a man came running up to the security station and excitedly reported that there was a dead man under a truck nearby. Everyone present hurriedly went to the truck where they did, indeed, find a man lying underneath it. But instead of being a dead man it turned out to be Emmett Eastman, a popular dancer who served on the Mdewakanton Advisory Committee. He was trying to get a good night's sleep. Emmett is very light on his feet and it is great fun to watch him dance. He is a frequent dancer at the Powwow. Although he was approaching old age when I first met him, he was still a marathon runner. He was famous for his running, having literally circumvented the globe as much as that can be done, and he had often led the runners at the Memorial Run in December.

Sitting around a campfire seems to promote storytelling. Some exceptionally tall tales can be heard. For example, Rose Crooks, now deceased, was one of the founders of the powwow in Mankato and came to this event every year with a huge RV. She was fairly old and had suffered a series of strokes that put her in a motorized chair. Every evening she would abandon the comforts of her expensive RV and come to my camp for the pleasures of sitting around the fire and telling stories and hearing the stories others would tell. In fact, she was there sometimes for most of the day.

One of the stories that Rose told was about the time her husband, Amos, had been pulled over by a traffic cop for speeding. He didn't have a driver's license at all, but before the patrolman got to the car, Amos quickly persuaded Rose to let him borrow hers. He gave her driver's license to the patrolman as if it were his own. This was a long time ago, before driver's licenses had pictures on them.

The officer checked the name on the card, looked at Amos, and said, "Rosemma Crooks. Is that you?"

Amos replied, "Yes, but it's not pronounced like that. It's Ross-e-ma, with the accent on the first syllable. It's a traditional Indian name."

"Ross-e-ma," the officer repeated. "Well, Ross-e-ma, you were going a little fast back there and I'm going to have to cite you." He wrote out the ticket, and Amos even went to court claiming to be Ross-e-ma. He paid his fine and got by with that. He never had to own up to not having a driver's license. Of course, Rosemma had a speeding ticket on her driving record, but that wouldn't have surprised anyone even though she didn't drive much. Rose didn't care much for rules.

Chapter Eleven

Spiritual Experiences

The Owl's Announcement of Gertrude Wells's Passing

During the wee hours of the morning while a few people still sat around my campfire telling stories and reflecting on the events of the day before. Leonard Wabasha and Richard Milda came by to chat and sample Beverly's cookies with some coffee. It had been a long day for everyone and it was their first opportunity to sit back and relax by the warm fire with casual conversation. It was a quiet, very pleasant moment. Just then, an owl hooted several times nearby. To the Dakota, an owl is a messenger of death. Sometimes the owl's hooting is an omen that death is near and someone is about to die. Sometimes it's a message that someone has died. In either case the message softens the blow and signals that some prayers should be offered. There was a long pause in the conversation and the owl hooted again.

Then someone, either Leonard or Richard, commented, "That's Gertrude."

The comment stimulated discussion of the fact that Gertrude Wells was in a hospital at the time and was not expected to live much longer. In the morning, news came that Gertrude had died during the night. Her death had occurred at the approximate time we heard the owl hooting. Most of us were quite surprised and very much impressed, but Richard Milda and Leonard Wabasha were neither surprised nor impressed. They seemed to view such matters as routine occurrences.

* * *

MANY THINGS HAPPEN at the powwow that eventually and inevitably quell skepticism about spirits and American Indian spirituality. For example, one time a beautiful, mature, bald eagle swooped down right over the dance arena during a dance while the drum was beating loudly and hundreds of dancers were in the arena and hundreds of spectators watched. An eagle would not be expected to do that ordinarily, but I saw it happen. It flew very low over the crowd of spectators and dancers and drumming at a mere forty feet above the ground. At its lowest point it dropped a large eagle feather, which fluttered down and landed right in the middle of the arena. Then the eagle flew off. When the eagle feather landed on the ground the drumming and dancing stopped and there was a long moment of silence.

Then four Dakota elders surrounded the feather and said some prayers. Finally, one of the elders reached down and picked up the beautiful eagle feather. Then the drumming and dancing started again. This reverence for eagle feathers is in strict accordance with Dakota traditions. When an eagle feather is found on the ground, only an elder or sacred pipe carrier can pick it up. This was a very meaningful thing. From any perspective, it was a very spiritual occurrence. Many believed the eagle was delivering a message from the Great Spirit and the feather was a prized award to the powwow as a whole, perhaps reflecting the Great Spirit's approval of the event.

* * *

Purification Ceremonies (Sweats)

MUCH OF WHAT FOLLOWS regarding purification ceremonies is reproduced from the author's book, *While God Was Hidden*.

On Thursday afternoon Bill Gilbert and his brother approached me to ask where they could find some small willows so they could build a sweat lodge. I told them I knew some were growing on my own property and they could have them, but I would have to go with them to get them because they'd never find them on their own. They were on some river bottom property I owned in St Peter, about twenty miles away. We started out, all three of us squeezing into the cab of my little Ford Ranger. We had traveled only a few miles when they spotted willows just outside of Mankato. They were near Steve Hiniker's sawmill, so I drove to the mill to ask if the land was his and if we could cut some. He said it wasn't his land but we could just go ahead and cut some because nobody would care. They grew like weeds and were on highway right-of-way—essentially public property. So we went to get them.

My Ranger had four-wheel drive, so I drove through the ditch and right up to the thicket of willows. We all got out and entered the thicket. Bill found the largest willow around. He took some tobacco and rubbed the trunk of the four-inch tree with handfuls of it as he said some prayers in Dakota.

Then, in English, for my benefit I presume, he said, "Forgive us, Grandfather, for we are going to take many of your grandchildren. I want you to know that they will be treated with great respect and will become part of a sacred lodge. We are very grateful for them."

After another couple of prayers in Dakota, we proceeded to cut some tall willows, which grew abundantly all around us. The young trees were only about an inch in diameter. Bill and his brother cut the willows, selecting them for their size, while I bundled them up and carried one load after another to the truck. Willows of that small size grew to about fifteen feet tall in the middle of that thicket. They were nice and straight and green. I could carry a half dozen at a time. We cut about twenty of them. Bill said they were perfect for our purpose.

We then returned to the site for the sweat lodge and began to build the lodge. I had the task of stripping the bark from some of the willows. They had me cut strips as long as possible so the bark strips could be used to tie the willow poles together for the framework of the lodge. While I worked at stripping the bark from the poles, I watched as others punched carefully located holes in the ground into which the lodge poles were inserted. When the circle of poles was established, the poles were bent over and tied together with the bark strips, completing the dome-like frame for the lodge structure. This was reinforced with willows tied horizontally, making the whole framework very sturdy. All that remained to complete the lodge was to cover it with large pieces of canvas.

I learned a lot in helping to build that sweat lodge. I am confident now that, if ever I was lost in the woods when hiking or hunting, I can build a shelter for protection from the elements with materials invariably on hand. It is a comforting feeling to be confident that I could use this knowledge for survival in the wilderness should that become necessary.

More than just the lodge is required, however, for the sweat ceremony. When covering the lodge, a doorway into it is established on the west side. Inside the lodge, a small excavation is dug in the middle to accommodate the hot rocks for the sweat. Perhaps twenty feet west of the doorway a fire is started to heat the rocks for the sweat. The rocks are piled into a pit at that location and the fire is built on top of them. The rocks are specially selected field stones and, when hot, are called "Grandfathers."

An altar is established and located between the fire and the door to the lodge. The altar, as I observed it, contained a buffalo skull, tobacco, sage, sweet grass, cedar greens, the Owen family bundle, and the Mdewakanton Club staff. I'm sure that the composition of the altar varies depending on the spiritual leader conducting the sweat. At some point a "spirit plate" is placed upon the altar with a sampling of the foods provided to the dancers. All of this is considered sacred after being blessed by the spiritual leader. It is never left unattended and no pictures are allowed.

The tools of the sweat ceremony include a bucket of water, a pitchfork to carry the white-hot stones from the fire to the door of the lodge, and a deer antler with which to rake the hot stones onto the pile in the middle of the lodge. The spiritual leader sprinkles the stones with water to heat the lodge when the ceremony starts. He sprinkles on some sweet grass clippings or sage or tobacco or cedar or a mixture of those things.

When no more sweats are to be held in the lodge, it must be ritualistically disassembled and returned to Mother Earth. This is accomplished by burning the framework in the spirit fire used to heat the rocks for the sweat. On Monday morning, long after most people have already headed for home, it is routine to see many devotees of American Indian spirituality busily working at the site of the sweat ceremony, taking care of the lodge by burning it and cleaning up the area where the sweat ceremony was held. The rituals include prayers to the Great Spirit (Wakan Tonka). Then the dance arena or circle is "closed" and the powwow officially ends. The sweat lodge is returned to Mother Earth and the arena, when closed, is no longer sacred until the next time it is blessed.

* * *

HAVING BEEN BORN INTO A CATHOLIC family I was an altar boy for a while in my youth, but eventually I rejected Christianity entirely for a number of reasons not relevant here. After that I was skeptical of everything that smacked of any kind of spirituality. I remained skeptical of every kind of religious and spiritual belief and anything supernatural for most of my adult life until I became involved with the American Indians (Dakota) at the Mankato Powwow. That happened after I had heard about the good Doctor W.W. Mayo, the father of the famous Mayo brothers, having taken the body of Cut Nose from the grave after the hanging of the thirty-eight Dakota in Mankato in 1862. All of the other bodies were stolen as well.

The first time I heard about the grave robbery was on a local radio station. A talk show commentator expressed some astonishment at the story, and that got my attention. But then I didn't hear anything more about it for quite some time. Still, the story stuck in my mind. Whenever I came across the few bits of information revelant to this, my base of information grew and my interest with it.

The more I learned about the war in 1862 between the American Indians and the white settlers, the more interesting it became. For a while, the story seemed to become more absurd and incredible with each new bit of information I collected. When I began to look into the historical accounts of these events more earnestly, reading all I could find in the local library, I was astonished to find that many of the "absurdities" were well-documented facts. The old axiom, "Truth is stranger than fiction," is vividly realized in this history.

I first joined the Mdewakanton Association as a way of learning more about the American Indians and possibly learning more about Cut Nose, one of the leaders in the 1862 war for whom I had a special interest. Through my membership in the association and through participation in various association activities, I learned a lot more about the American Indians, but most of what I learned about Cut Nose came from library research, books, and old newspapers. Through my years of membership in the association, I had the questionable pleasure of serving as the president for two years and past-president for three more. However, most of the work I did for the association was laboring on the grounds crew at the annual powwow, getting things in place, hauling wood, problem solving, and taking out the garbage. Despite this sometimes demeaning work, I enjoyed the friendship of the people I worked with. Although I was not looking for spiritual experiences, some of the most interesting experiences I had there were absolutely spiritual. Gradually, through these experiences, I came to acknowledge that there are spirits, and I have acquired a strong belief and a lot of interest in American Indian spirituality.

Membership in the Mdewakanton Association opened some doors for me in the Dakota culture. I had the unquestionable pleasure of meeting some of the most interesting people I have ever met in my entire life. Some of these have become close and dear friends. And on three occasions I attended a "sweat," a spiritual ceremony in some ways like a sauna that involved a lot of praying. But a sauna and a sweat are not even in the same ballpark.

Each year, on the Thursday evening before the powwow, the members of the Mdewakanton Association meet to discuss last-minute details of preparations. This is a big meeting with all the members of the association attending, perhaps thirty people. Some of the Dakota at the meeting say prayers, appealing to the Great Spirit for a good powwow. All those attending are "smoked," or smudged with smoke from a plate of smoldering sage. This sacred purification rite helped to set the mood for the powwow, helped a person enter into it seriously, and helped put a person's heart in the right place, helping to ensure the success of the powwow.

It was after that meeting on Thursday evening, September 17, 1992, when my brother-in-law, Roger Elfrink, and I decided that we would go to the "sweat" to which I had been invited as a new member of the association. Roger's invitation came from me because I wanted some familiar company when there. At that time, I had been told a sweat was something like a sauna. Roger loved a sauna so it wasn't hard to convince him to go even though he wasn't very well prepared for this in that he would have to go in his undershorts. Several of the association members had urged me to go, saying things like, "Oh, if you've never been to one, you should go. You'll enjoy it. You'll come out feeling very relaxed and refreshed. You'll be re-juvenated." Eventually, I agreed to attend and asked Roger to go with me.

The sweat lodge was located in a secluded spot down near the confluence of the Blue Earth and Minnesota rivers, away from the dance arena and past the camping areas. When the time came to go, about 10:30 p.m., I was quite tired and really wanted to back out, but then, Bev (my soul mate), and Cheryl (my sister and Roger's wife), insisted that both Roger and I go. I put on some shorts, and Roger and I headed in the general direction of the lodge, not knowing its exact location. We soon found it, as there was a big hardwood fire right in front of it. Roger and I had delivered some good hardwood there earlier in the day, but I hadn't realized that the sweat lodge was right there next to the woodpile. Now it made sense to me. Where else would it be?

The fire was very hot, a pile of blazing logs about three feet high, and the guys tending it kept stoking it. I couldn't help but think they were going to go through a lot of wood at that rate. I calculated that the rocks for the sweat must be under those coals. A dozen guys stood around the fire. Nobody said anything. They were just concentrating on the fire. I went to talk with one of the American Indians I knew, Bob the Cutter, who was a cousin of our arena director. He had accompanied me when we delivered about 640 pounds of donated buffalo meat to a cooler at a restaurant in town (the management having agreed to keep it on ice for us). I don't recall what I said to Bob the Cutter, but his response ignored my comment. He explained that it was his custom to study the fire, meditate, open his mind, and get in the mood for the sweat before entering. It was clear he didn't want to talk, and he was also modeling for me what I needed to do to prepare for the sweat.

That's what everyone was doing, standing around the fire, concentrating on it, meditating, and I became aware then that this was no ordinary sauna. There was an altar behind the fire consisting of a small pile of things topped off by the buffalo skull, which I knew was considered by the Dakota to be a sacred object. I knew, also, that somewhere in that pile was the Owens's family "bundle," quite literally a bundle of items of great significance to the family, their most treasured possessions and relics. When he died, Amos Owen passed this on to his son, Ray, who for a long time had been recognized as the one who would likely follow in his father's footsteps to become a spiritual leader in his own right. Ray didn't just step into his father's shoes and the role of spiritual leader when his father died. At age eleven he had been accidentally electrocuted when he touched a power line while climbing a tree. He survived this experience, one that would have killed most people. After that he was thought to be "special," not in any negative way, but in many positive ways. His survival convinced him and everyone around him that the Great Spirit had saved him for special purposes. He studied and learned as much as he could about American Indian spirituality, learning much from his father, of course, but learning from other sources also. Today, he is an acknowledged spiritual leader, not just because he is the son of Amos Owen, but because of his own personal accomplishments as well.

Ray was present and in charge of this sweat, which was intended to be a ceremony to "call in" the spirits of the thirty-eight warriors who had been hanged in Mankato after the Sioux Uprising of 1862. Prominently displayed at the altar was a staff of thirty-eight eagle feathers representing the thirty-eight warriors hanged. There were two more feathers on the staff representing two other American Indians who were hanged, but those two feathers were attached to the staff separately because those two Dakota chiefs (Shakopee and Medicine Bottle) were hanged at another time at Fort Snelling.

One of Ray's assistants, Keith Reynolds, was gesticulating about the altar, waving a small drum about, occasionally beating a few times on it, and once in a while he would chant some phrases. He continued in this manner for some time, perhaps fifteen minutes. Like the others, I stood with Roger and quietly watched the fire while this assistant kept beating on the drum and going through some traditional rituals.

Except for the sounds of this preliminary ceremony, it was a quiet time. Some guys were getting ready to enter the sweat lodge, removing their clothes, and putting them in a pile with their eyeglasses on top.

Brad Hardt, president of the Mdewakanton Association at the time, came over to Roger and me and quietly whispered instructions: "Don't wear anything metal. It'll get too hot. Leave your glasses out here. When you enter the door of the sweat be sure to say, 'All my relatives.' If you have to leave during the ceremony be sure to crawl around the pit. You will have to cross people's legs to avoid the hot rocks. Don't touch the rocks. They'll burn you."

Ray Owen took over the ritualizing and the ceremony began in earnest. He said some prayers, some in English and some in Dakota. At that point, I heard a roaring in the treetops like I had heard before in the woods up north when I was deer hunting, only much, much louder, and growing louder still. In fact, the sound became so loud it was a lot like a formation of about six jet fighter planes approaching at about fifty feet above the trees. Then the sound stopped very abruptly. Incredibly, nobody else seemed to take notice.

I nudged Roger and whispered, "Did you hear that?"

He listened a long moment and said, "What?"

"I heard a roar up in the trees," I said.

He listened again, then said, "Oh, you mean that motorcycle?"

I listened then and, sure enough, there was a motorcycle revving up repeatedly over in the camp area. The sound was like, "Brrrruuumm, Brrrruuumm, Brrrruuumm."

I was extremely skeptical and thought, *Well, it certainly couldn't have been just that motorcycle*, trying hard to reconcile what I had heard with some reasonable representation in reality. After all, a motorcycle doesn't compare with six jets at treetop level. The praying continued. I looked around, noticing the sweat lodge behind the altar, and noticing, too, that there was something strange going on with the feathers on the staff of thirty-eight eagle feathers that was part of the altar.

Again I nudged Roger and whispered, "Watch the feathers."

There was more praying, and some songs were sung in the Dakota language. I was surprised that most of those present seemed to know the words. But I was more surprised by what the feathers seemed to be doing. I couldn't take my eyes off them. It appeared that instead of hanging down the side of the staff as feathers were supposed to do, they were all standing straight out from the staff as if a strong wind were blowing them. But there was no strong wind, and they were all in a perfect rigid line, not wavering as they might if a wind were blowing them. Moreover, they seemed to point first at one of the men present, then at another, all the feathers moving simultaneously from one man to another, like they were looking as a group at each of us, pausing slightly at each man standing in a semicircle around the fire. When the feathers paused on me, I marveled at how they were so perfectly lined up. They pointed in the direction of every man, moving sometimes a little to the left, then a lot to the right, then a little left again, and so on until they had paused at every man. To do that, the feathers had to traverse more than 180 degrees. At the time, I thought that was strange because the air was calm, but still I didn't get excited about it.

Nor did I get excited when, just before we entered the sweat lodge, the feathers made a perfect spiral, about a turn and a half, right up the staff. It was like the staff was saying something in a gesture that I understood at the time to mean something like, "Okay boys, come on in."

I have since learned that the eagle feather staff is constructed so that all of the feathers are tied together and held straight out by the tie. That would explain why all the feathers moved together as an unwavering unit, but it would not account for the movement of the feathers from one man to another when there was no wind. And furthermore, tied together as they were, it was not even possible for the feathers to have made a spiral-like gesture as they did.

Crawling into the sweat lodge, I forgot, of course, to say, "All my relatives," which is required, almost like a ticket to enter. Someone in the dark by the door prompted me to do that. I said it and then proceeded to crawl through the dark around the edge of the lodge to where those before me had piled up. Others, including Roger, followed me. Soon the lodge was full, and I got the impression that just enough people showed up for this, as many as could be accommodated, and no more. About twenty guys sat around the edge of the lodge facing the center. I had a very good position which enabled me to look closely at the doorway to my left and take in all the action of the spiritual leader who sat next to the door.

When everyone was seated, the hot rocks were brought into the lodge and raked into the pit in the center one at a time. I think it must have been Keith bringing the rocks, getting them out of the hot coals of the fire with a pitchfork and bringing them to the doorway of the lodge on the tines of the fork. The rocks were laid on the ground in the doorway of the lodge and from there they were raked into the pit. I think it was Art Owen (Ray's brother) kneeling inside the lodge next to the doorway and raking the rocks with a deer antler.

Each rock was glowing red hot, was rolled with the antler across the ground to the pit, and rolled on the pile of those hot rocks already there. Ray Owen was seated on the other side of the door opening. Every time a new rock was put on the pile he would scatter something on it. This would sparkle as it hit the hot rock and the lodge filled with a peculiar fragrance from the smoke. It wasn't the smell of sweet grass and not like incense or a bonfire either. This was a strange odor to me, one I had not smelled before and have not smelled since. I don't know what it was.

Often, as a rock was brought in, one or more of the men in the lodge would shout "How!" or "Ho!" and add a couple of Dakota words, all of which seemed from context to have the meaning of something like, "Oh, wow, that's a good one!"

After about a dozen rocks were brought in one at a time, Art instructed the guy with the pitchfork to bring two at a time, apparently to hasten the process. On the next trip back from the fire there were two rocks on the tines of the fork. As the fork was lowered to put them on the ground one of the rocks fell off and rolled into the side of the lodge at the edge of the doorway. These rocks were glowing yellowish-red hot and would surely cause serious injury to anyone who touched them or was touched by them. The loose, hot rock caused some brief excitement and what sounded like cursing among the people nearest the door, even including our spiritual leader, I think. I'm not certain they were cursing because the words were in Dakota, and I understood that the Dakota language contains no curse words, but the angry tone was definitely suggestive of cursing. Art soon had the loose rock raked into the pit and the potential emergency was over. No serious damage had been done.

As soon as all the twenty-one rocks were piled into the pit, a bucket of water was placed inside the door and the door flap was closed. The lodge was then absolutely dark except for a bright glow of the rocks. The heat grew very intense as soon as the door was closed, but it increased dramatically when the spiritual leader began to sprinkle water on the rocks. The lodge quickly filled with steam. I began to sweat almost immediately. This caused some difficulty because my skin became slippery. I had my arms wrapped around my knees, holding my legs up near my body to keep my feet out of the hot rocks. This was not easy to do in the first place, but it became a lot more difficult when my grip on my legs became slippery. I shifted positions, but none were very satisfactory, and at once I began to look forward to the end of this ordeal although it had just begun.

Ray Owen kept up his praying and his sprinkling, and it kept getting hotter, and my skin got sweatier and even more slippery. The rocks even seemed to get hotter as time passed. Occasionally, a rock would seem to crackle with a spray of sparks, or perhaps it was merely something combustible that the spiritual leader threw on the fire. In the darkness, he could have done that without being seen. On one occasion an incredible display of sparks briefly lit up a small area of the lodge and lasted for a while. All the while during the sweat ceremony many tiny bluish glowing specks seemed to float about in the air inside the lodge. The prayers spoken in English had to do with ancestors, their sufferings, and how meager are the sufferings that we must endure, comparatively speaking.

More Dakota songs were sung, and again I was surprised at how many of those present knew both the words and the melodies. Brad Hardt had to exit because his lungs became congested. Before he actually left, the spiritual leader suggested he try lying down. I wondered how anyone would lie down in this crowd, but Brad apparently tried that and found no relief. When the door was opened to let him out, a welcome gush of cool air gave all of us some relief. Roger, who loved a sauna, was next to go. The spiritual leader prayed that these brothers (I think he actually referred to them as "babies") would be strengthened, their weaknesses overcome, or words to that effect. He actually seemed to be trying to humiliate them. At least, that was my impression.

Toward the end I was convinced that this whole affair was more of an endurance test than something one would do for the pleasure of it. There was no immediate pleasure I could discern, except for those among us who might have had a high measure of masochism in our makeup. I would learn later that it is the spiritual quality and the effects of the sweat that may be pleasurable. But when I stop to think about it, perhaps getting purified, getting evil removed from one's being, might be expected to be somewhat painful.

The heat became searing. I covered my face with my towel to protect myself from the radiance of the hot rocks, but the steam penetrated everything. Once or twice, I felt as if a few stray drops of the sprinkled water hit me. I assumed then that the spiritual leader was sprinkling more water on the rocks. Probably less than one tenth of one percent of my body surface was cooled, but even that was immensely appreciated. In retrospect, this sensation of cooling could have been a brush by spirits in the sweat lodge with us. I had my mind made up that if another opportunity would arise for me to leave the lodge without disturbing the ceremony too much, I would do it, whether or not I'd look like a weakling. At this late stage in life, I was not at all worried about my masculinity. Many of those still in the lodge were making noises that sounded like plaintive moans, groans, and grunts, and I suspected that many would have left with me. But then the ceremony ended and everyone filed out of the lodge on their hands and knees.

Once outside, everyone collapsed. Brad and Roger were out there, both looking quite relieved. The air was cool and refreshing. I remembered how the air had felt almost uncomfortably cool before the sweat, but now I would not have objected if the temperature dropped ten degrees, which it might well have done during the hour-long sweat. The air felt wonderful. I put my wet towel on the ground and lay down upon it. I looked up through the branches of the nearby trees silhouetted against an incredibly starlit sky. The leaves on the trees were motionless as the air was absolutely calm.

Without considering the questionable quality of my remark, I said, for the benefit of all within earshot, "Wow! If I wasn't a redskin before I went in there, I probably am now!" The way I felt, I thought I probably looked like a steamed lobster—at least that's what I had in mind. I didn't think that "redskin" was a derogatory term among American Indians. I gave it no thought before I said it, or I would not have used that term at all. Someone might have been offended by that remark, but nobody said anything, literally. Everyone lay quietly, silently, not moving or saying anything. I now know that chatting it up following the sweat was not appropriate behavior. This was a time to meditate and privately reflect on the ceremony just completed.

After a while I got up to leave and went over to the woodpile where I had stashed my eyeglasses and boots. Quite a number of people were lying around in the dark there. As I picked up my things and started to leave I made a little speech. I don't know now what possessed me then, but I said (as I recall), "Once again I have learned that one can have too much of a good thing. I feel like a teenager, drunk for the first time, having liked and enjoyed the beer and whiskey, but not knowing when to quit. Nevertheless, I enjoyed the sweat and found the whole experience to be quite marvelous. Thank you all very much for permitting me to share it with you."

I carried my boots and walked barefoot with Roger back to the "Silver Bullet" (that's what the Dakota called my Airstream camping trailer) where Bev and Cheryl were waiting for us. Roger and Cheryl went home immediately. They were tired. I got dressed and went down to the cook shack just to complete the experience of having gone to a sweat. All of the participants at a sweat were supposed to go to the cook shack afterward for a late-night snack, was my understanding. That part of it isn't worth much comment, in my opinion. One guy from the sweat was there before me. I had some juice and a bowl of buffalo soup. The soup had very little substance to it. It had some pieces of buffalo, but practically no vegetables and it was thin and watery. The others were just coming as I left to go back to the Silver Bullet. Bev was in bed and I crawled in with her.

She asked, "Did anything interesting happen at the sweat?"

"I'll tell you later," I said as I quickly went to sleep.

The Ghost Dancers

On Sunday the powwow ends. At least that's when most people go home. Some of the concessions close up early, but the powwow in Mankato is the last of the season in Minnesota and for some vendors it is the last of the year. Some go on to other powwows in warmer climes, where powwows are put on all year. Most of the dancers leave on Sunday too, many sticking around for the last dance that usually occurs just before sunset.

The sun had just dipped below the horizon at the end of one powwow in the early 1990s when a small, impromptu club meeting took place at the Silver Bullet, my camp, to review the events, plan the cleanup, and get organized for stowing all our gear. Someone at the meeting noticed that a thick fog had settled over the circle and called everyone's attention to it.

"Look at that fog! It's just over the arena. There's no fog anywhere else. Isn't that strange?"

Everyone looked at the fog. Sure enough, it was like a thin cloud covering the dance circle. It was impossible to see through it, but it seemed as if there were swirling figures within it, like there were dancers moving around out there. The group at the meeting stared in amazement at this fog for some time as it faded or lifted and disappeared completely, revealing that no one was there.

Everyone was in awe. A fog covering all of the dance circle and nothing else did not seem like a natural thing. Nothing like that had happened before. The fog had appeared so quickly, and then disappeared so quickly, nobody quite knew what to make of it.

There were comments like, "Did you see that?" "I saw something, but I'm not sure what it was." "It looked like there were dancers out there." "There *were* dancers out there. Maybe they were ghost dancers."

Then someone noticed another fog, this time quite a distance away, down in a corner of the treeline across the parking area. It looked like the same one that had been over the circle, as if it had moved from the arena to that more distant place.

"Hey, would you look at that! There it is again."

This time it was too far away to see anything inside of it. Everyone saw the cloud and just watched silently as it, too, faded away quite quickly. The people were alert to anything more that might happen, but that was it. They talked about it, and all were in agreement that something unusual had just occurred, but they were not quite sure what had happened. Was it merely an illusion? Was it the spirits of the thirty-eight having a good time? These observations seemed at least to have opened the minds of some of these people to the possibility that something spiritual had happened. And one or two of the witnesses to this spectacle were certain that the powwow had just been visited by spirits.

For clarification, the reference to "ghost dancers" was, in this context, an expression having the meaning or connotation that the perceived dancers were not real live people dancing in the fog, but rather were spirits, ghostly figures. The term "ghost dancers" was applied long ago (1890, 1891) to American Indian dancers who engaged in spiritual dancing despite the efforts of white men to suppress and forbid such activity.[1]

In a recent conversation with Vernell Wabasha, she told me a story that was, for me, quite astonishing. We were discussing the efforts that went into promoting and managing the early powwows when she recalled feeling lonely when the powwow ended. She said that the powwows were a lot of fun for her in those days despite all the hard work that went into them. On one such occasion, when almost everyone had gone home, she was sitting at a campfire with the few people who remained and someone drew their attention to the fog that had settled over the dance arena. It was like a thin cloud just over the arena and not anywhere else. Not only that, but there seemed to be dancers in it.

Someone said, "Maybe it's the spirits of the thirty-eight doing their appreciation dance."

They all saw it and watched for a while. Nobody said anything more. Then the fog dissipated and was gone, the dancers with it.

When something like that happens, I have a tendency to do some reality testing. "What's going on here," I might ask myself. "Did that really happen or is my imagination running away with me?" Hearing this story from Vernell about the same thing happening twenty years earlier to different people made me feel a lot more confident about my own experience. It was almost exactly the same. Vernell's story served to make mine more acceptable and credible.

Extra Honor Guards

IF ONE IS WILLING TO APPROACH PEOPLE at the powwow and engage in conversation, a lot can be learned and some very interesting characters met. For example, during the 2010 Powwow I was having a casual conversation with two members of the honor guard whom I had just met after a grand entry ceremony. I learned that one of them, Brad Nelson, had been born in my home town, Willmar, Minnesota, and we had some mutual acquaintances. The other guy, Mike Greeley, was an American Indian and turned out to be a great-great-grandson of Little Crow, chief of the American Indians in the 1862 War. Both of these guys were veterans of the Vietnam War.

Mike Greeley told me a very interesting story. During the Mankato Powwow of the previous year (2009) both he and Brad had participated in a demonstration of a "night patrol." In this demonstration all the lights of the dance arena were turned off and the soldiers of the honor guard, dressed in combat fatigues and carrying arms, went around the arena in a crouched posture, pointing their rifles one way, then another way, and occasionally firing off a round or two (blanks, of course). Nobody was supposed to take pictures during this demonstration, but one young lady apparently took one, the flash lighting up the whole arena. Someone stopped her from taking more pictures, and after the demonstration ended she approached the members of the honor guard to apologize for causing a disturbance. She also showed the guards the picture she had taken. When they looked at it they were astounded because, according to both Mike and Brad, in the picture were images of soldiers in the night patrol who were not a part of their group. I remembered seeing that demonstration and I recalled that there were more soldiers in the demonstration than the six or eight members of the honor guard. Both Mike and Brad became choked up and a little tearful as they told me that they believed the extra images were the spirits of soldiers they had served with in Vietnam, men who did not make it out of there alive. I told them I'd give my right arm to see that picture, but neither of them knew the girl or where she came from or where she went.

Brushes

MANY TIMES I HAVE BEEN "BRUSHED" BY SPIRITS. That's what the American Indians call it. I didn't know what being brushed was until after it happened to me a couple of times and I talked to some American Indians about it. They say it is one of the many ways the spirits let you know of their presence. One kind of brush is an inexplicable feeling of coolness on a part of one's body, such as the upper arm, or perhaps the cheek. Describing one is difficult. It is a strange feeling because of the inexplicable quality of it. That makes a description of it easier by describing what it isn't. For example, one might feel cool on a certain localized part of the body because of a peculiar breeze, like a tiny fan might make, but there isn't necessarily any air movement connected with a brush. It's not like being cooled by a fan. It's not being cooled by a movement of air. And it doesn't come from within oneself. It's definitely on the outside of the skin. It's not like entering into a bubble of cool air, either, because more often than not, it happens when one is not entering into anything, but merely standing or sitting motionless. It's not for everyone. A single person in a crowd can be brushed while the rest of the crowd feels nothing —yet several people in a group can be brushed simultaneously. It's a little like approaching something cool, like a block of ice, and feeling the drop in temperature that surrounds the ice, but the feeling is very localized on the body. It's impossible to explain by the most customary analyses of stimulus and response.

* * *

MANY THINGS HAPPEN AT THE POWWOW that have a spiritual quality. The spirits seem to abound there. For example, a young woman told me that at the grand entry on Saturday of the 2010 Powwow, she was watching the activities from the bleachers when she glanced over her shoulder to the northeast and saw, over the trees, a fog or haze. That caught her eye because it was not a foggy or hazy day. As she looked at it, something extremely unusual appeared within it. A bald eagle was soaring around in there, holding a long-stemmed rose in its talons. After thinking about it and puzzling about it for a time, she came to believe that this was not only the spirit of Amos Crooks (whose Indian name was "Eagle Boy") but also the spirit of his wife, Rosemma, whom everyone called Rose. When the young lady looked at the haze a second time, she saw the form of a bear. This made her recall that another close American Indian friend, the late Sharynn Baker, was of the bear clan, and it would not be surprising that she would be in the company of Amos and Rose, for in life they were all very good, close friends. She then looked back at the dancing and then back at the haze a third time. This time she saw the eagle with the rose in his talons soaring as before, and the bear trailing behind, running with the eagle. She looked away briefly, and when she looked again for the haze and the spirits within it they had all faded away completely.

Notes

1. Mails, p. 586.

Epilogue

THE MANKATO POWWOW has had some success in reconciling the relationships between the American Indians and the white communities, but there is still much to be done. The reconciliation work must continue. More powwows are needed and more are planned. Despite all that has been accomplished, more education and forgiveness on both sides would be helpful. Many of the descendents of the settlers who were killed in 1862 still harbor grudges against the Dakota, and many of the Dakota are still suffering from the abuses to which their ancestors were subjected and which they, too, have more recently suffered.

The year 2012 marks the 150th anniversary of the 1862 War and the hanging in Mankato of the thirty-eight Dakota warriors. Planning for the 2012 Powwow includes some special ceremonies to recognize the 150th anniversary and, hopefully, to help put an end to all the unhealthy and uncomfortable feelings associated with the 1862 War and its aftermath.

Whoever said, "Time heals all wounds" did not know the whole truth. Sometimes, time merely postpones what needs to be done for the healing to be accomplished, perpetuating the pains resulting from those wounds, perhaps even for generations. Time also tends to blur the lines of the details of the wounding, distorting them until they become less recognizable, less real, perhaps even less honest. Time sometimes covers the truth with cobwebs and dust in thick layers, which somehow enables us to overlook the truth or ignore it and make claims that it is something that it is not. It enables us to claim that "we didn't do it" so it becomes "not our problem." While it may be true that we did not cause the wounds that give others pain, those wounds sometimes become a part of who we are, part of the fabric of our lives.

We have all heard that two wrongs do not make a right. Well, many more wrongs than two were committed during the 1862 War between the whites and the

Dakota, some merely cruel and deceitful, some illegal, and some were downright unthinkable atrocities committed by *both sides*. Some of the sufferings from those wrongs committed so long ago have continued through many generations and are still present today, especially among the Dakota, in the form of bitterness, poverty, hatred, alcoholism, in broken social structures within the Dakota nation, in physical, emotional, and sexual abuses, and in crime and even suicidal behavior.

"So what?" we might ask. Why should we care? We were not responsible—we did not, ourselves, commit the wrongful deeds. Such denial does not pass the sniff test. And does that kind of denial mean that the whites do not suffer in the aftermath all these years later? Much to the contrary, many white people whose ancestors were terrorized or killed by the Dakota in the 1862 War are still hurting and full of hate because of that. In this sesquicentennial year, the 150th anniversary of the war and hanging, there has been a surge of letters to the editor of the *Mankato Free Press* about the war, the hanging, and the monuments commemorating them. In some, the American Indians are called murderers and rapists. But all of that pain and antagonism is fruitless and even destructive. The flurry of letters to the *Free Press* are strong evidence that more reconciliation is needed. So what can be done to end it? The consequences of grief and loss are such that it is difficult to see an end to it. But, where there is grief and loss, there is also room for strength and healing.

The wrongs committed in 1862 before, during, and after the War were committed by both sides of the War and have not been completely corrected. They cannot be, but the genocidal acts of the United States against the American Indians and the slaughter of the settlers are history and must be put behind us. They should not be forgotten, but they must not be allowed to continue to cause pain.

Because the most horrible things done in the 1862 War happened 150 years ago, we now can view them from a distance and with more objectivity. Time can be on our side. We can brush away the cobwebs and wipe away the dust to examine those horrors more clearly. We can educate ourselves to learn why those awful things occurred and we can understand both sides of the conflict even better than if we had been directly involved. We can learn to recognize that both sides suffered great losses then and if we can learn to recognize the continuing negative results we can make peace, meaning more than just putting an end to the conflict. We can make peace within ourselves, too. We can eliminate the hatred and bigotry and turmoil that have existed for 150 years by acknowledging our own errors, the errors of the past and the present, and stop blaming anyone for them. "Harmony" is one meaning of the word, "Dakota." We all need to live in harmony. We all need to forgive our ancestors and ourselves for the errors of the past and live with peace and harmony in our lives in the present and in the future.

At a lecture in January 2012, at Gustavus Adolphus College in St Peter, Minnesota, the speaker, John Peacock, a nationally known American Indian educator, said that the word "reconciliation" is controversial. When asked what would be controversial about it, he responded with one word: "reparations." To a follow-up question about what reparations, he responded by saying, "The American Indians want their land back." Since the American Indians are highly unlikely to get much of their land back, there must be some alternative routes to reconciliation if it is ever to gain very significant ground.

The Mankato Powwow has been and will continue to be one of the paths to reconciliation. It has already helped the Dakota to return to Southern Minnesota and to feel welcome where there once was a bounty on their scalps. For the last forty years the Dakota have danced in harmony with members of the local community at the Mankato Powwow.

Another speaker also mentioned reconciliation at the same series of lectures in which John Peacock spoke. This was John LaBatte, a mixed-blood Dakota who lives in New Ulm, the most embattled town in the 1862 War. He talked of having ancestors from both sides of the war. He said that reconciliation is impossible because there will never be enough understanding and forgiveness on either side to accomplish it. And he might be correct in that assertion in the sense that the issues between the white communities and the American Indians might never be completely resolved and reconciliation might never be complete. But it is evident that reconciliation does not happen suddenly or all at once. It develops over time and in small increments. If reconciliation is never completed, it must be recognized that accomplishing even some reconciliation is a good thing. Time alone will not accomplish it. It requires an effort on both sides to make it happen. Education, understanding, and forgiveness are what bring it about.

Jerry Dearly, a frequent master of ceremonies at the Mankato Powwow and at other powwows all across the Midwest and elsewhere, said recently that he has seen reconciliation happening in Mankato. He has observed the Powwow over a period of many years and has appreciation for the changes that took place over that time. People are friendlier than they were. He has seen such changes in other places as well. He said, "Reconciliation is happening. No matter how you define it, every individual will see it differently. Some people have their own personal resentments that enter into it."

The seeds of reconciliation started by the founders of the powwow have taken hold. There have been thirty-eight powwows in Mankato and the thirty-ninth is in the preparation stage. There are prominent monuments to American Indians in downtown Mankato cooperatively placed there by the local community and American Indian communities. The Education Day Program established at the pow-wow in 1987 has continued every year since then and has had such success that it has been replicated in many other places. It can not be denied that the hard work of the Mdewakanton Association, the continuing cooperative support for the pow-wow from the local communities and the American Indian communities, the success of the Education Day Program, and the Mankato Powwow itself are all clear evi-dence that this Mankato Powwow is, in fact, a Reconciliation Powwow.

Postscript: The Powwow's Impact on the Author

THE MANKATO POWWOW HAS A POWERFUL effect on many people. The way it affects one person is different from how it affects others. After attending and helping with the powwow for many years, I have acquired a better understanding of American Indians and their culture, as would be expected, for that is part of the mission of the powwow. But the powwow has also affected me profoundly in ways that have resulted in very surprising and significant changes in my life. For example, most of my life I was a devout religious skeptic, declining to believe in any kind of spirituality at all. My experiences at the powwow have significantly changed part of that. Although I am still a believer in the natural order of the universe, I now believe that there is much more to the nat-ural order of the universe than I previously knew.

What I have referred to as "spiritual experiences" are events that involved spirits. For most of my life my belief in the natural order of the universe included the belief that anything spiritual was supernatural, but now I believe that spiritual events can very well be part of the natural order of the universe. There are undoubt-edly many laws of nature that we just have not learned about as yet. We simply do not know how an eagle or a dragonfly can represent the spirit of someone departed. We do not know how a person's mind, psyche, soul, or life could possibly continue to exist after the person's body has been so damaged or worn out that it ceases to function at all. All those intangible things within us while we are "alive" do seem to continue on by themselves after we are "dead," and that might be the natural order of things—we just do not know how it happens. But we see evidence of it happening, and some of that evidence is what has made a believer out of me.

I have come to believe that we are not humans on a spiritual journey, but instead we are spirits on a human journey. The body is temporary and merely visited by the spirit. When life, the spirit, leaves the body, the body is disposed of some-how—it matters little how. But the spirit endures longer than the body. I don't know how to prove that, but I believe it to be true.

I believe that it does happen. There are spirits. There is some kind of life after death. What we call death is not the loss of life but merely the demise of a functional body. Life goes on. When the body stops functioning, life leaves the body. This is nothing new. It seems that all the religions of the world believe this. As far back as I can remember, when reference is made to a deceased person I have heard people say, "He (or she) is gone." We call the person the "dearly departed." We talk as if the dead person is no longer there, "gone to a better place," but not as if the person has ceased to exist.

Since becoming involved with the powwow and with American Indian spirituality, I have not only come to believe in spirits, but I have come to view God quite differently. Most religions assert that the Creator of the universe is God, who started with nothing and built the universe from that. And where did He come from? Well, it is said that He "is, was, and always shall be." Some say the same thing about the universe—that it is, was, and always shall be. We know that energy is never used up, but just changes form. In creating the universe, God is thought to have started with a *tabula rasa*, a blank slate, and that He began to design the universe according to His own wishes. In fact, some of His creations do seem to be quite whimsical. The platypus, for example, is a furry mammal with webbed feet, a beaver tail, and a duck's bill that lays an egg, and when the egg hatches, the platypus nurses its offspring. If God is responsible for everything, then why are there so many different religions? If He is the Creator of everything, then is he not responsible for all the different beliefs? Is He playing some kind of capricious game for His own amusement with the different religions? Is He testing one religion against the others? Isn't it true that the differences between religions have been the cause of many wars and the deaths of many millions of human beings? Is that a good thing? What's it all about?

My thoughts about God are my own and I won't apologize for them, but I will say that I do not require anyone else to think about God as I do, and I do wish that my comments would not offend anyone. It is not my intention to be offensive to anyone. I do not mean to challenge the Bible or any other holy scripture or any of the reader's beliefs. I am merely relating the way it is with me, and the reader can believe whatever s/he wishes.

If one thinks about God as a deity with human-like form, then He could quite possibly have created the universe for His own amusement. It also could be possible that He becomes bored with his creations occasionally and He might be tempted to wipe them all out. It might be like erasing the blackboard so He could start all over if He wanted to do so. That would not be good from the human point of view. It is said that "God is good," but it is also said that everything that God does is good, so who is to say that He doesn't clear the board from time to time? He could take his time doing this with forty days and forty nights of rain flooding the entire world. He is said to have done this already, saving a couple of most species, but letting some species go, such as the dinosaurs. He could do it again very quickly with a giant asteroid or an exploding volcano, whatever might be his whim, or perhaps He has already done those things too. He is thought to be capable of anything.

If God created man in His own image, then would not God have the image of man? It is impossible for me to envision God as man-like in any way. Some religions refer to God as "God the Father," but most never mention any kind of mother. If God is man-like, there must be a mother. Does God get tired and does He sleep? Does He get hungry? What does He eat? If one considers all the ramifications of being man-like, then it becomes hard to believe that God is like that or that God created man in his own image.

I prefer to believe that God is not like man and I do believe that man is not at all like God. I cannot believe that God made man in his own image. It is certainly true that many men are anything but God-like. American Indian spirituality refers to God as "the Great Spirit," Wakan Tonka in Dakota. Sometimes American Indians call God "the Great Mystery." I like that. It is an acknowledgement that nobody has all the answers and there is still a lot to be learned. When envisioning the Great Spirit or the Great Mystery, one does not think of a man-like figure or any figure at all. I like that. The vision is more like a force, like the force of nature, like the combination of the natural forces of the universe, or perhaps even the entirety of the natural order of the universe itself, including all of mankind. And I like that.

As I grow older and approach the time when my body has endured all that it can and begins to wear out, I have noticed that time seems to pass by more quickly. Like in the song, sunrises are quickly followed by sunsets and one season quickly follows another. "Time slips away." This perception is not mine alone, but seems to be quite universal among old folks. And as the years go by, the passing of time seems to accelerate. Young people do not have this perception of time and are not even aware of it, but they usually become aware of it as they grow old. Nobody seems to object to the accelerated passage of time very strongly, perhaps because as the body wears out it becomes more and more difficult to inhabit. It grows weak and incapable of many of the activities of youth, and often full of pain.

With my new belief in spirituality I do not have great fear of the demise of my body. Instead, I can look forward to another continued existence. I am not sure what that new journey will be like, but it will be quite an adventure to find out what it is. I have attended American Indian funerals in which there were elaborate descriptions of what it is, but I think it is probably not the same for all spirits.

Few of the people who attend the powwow in Mankato will have the same response to it as I have had, but I think it's fair to say that most who attend the powwow will find it to be a very interesting and satisfying experience, and it is quite common for even first-time visitors at the powwow to have spiritual encounters quite similar to those I have had. There are ceremonies at the powwow that invite the spirits to come, and many spirits do attend. If you attend the powwow with an open mind, you, also, might meet some of them.

Summary of Historical Events

1912 Granite monument placed at hanging site.

1958 Bud Lawrence meets Wally Wells and Amos Owen.

1963 Mankato YMCA Indian Guide Program visited Prairie Island to attend a mini powwow.

1965 Bud Lawrence and Barry Blackhawk (accompanied in a car by Bob Rolfes and the sons of all) walk from Mankato to Prairie Island to honor Amos Owen's election as tribal chairman of the Prairie Island Community.

1965 The Prairie Island Tribal Council conducted a mini powwow and ceremony in the Mankato YMCA gym with Amos Owen, Wally Wells, Ed Jefferson, and Chris Leith presenting.

1969 Bud Lawrence and Jim Buckley walk from Mankato to Prairie Island to honor Amos Owen and the Prairie Island Community again.

1970 to 1985 Dakota Learning Opportunities established in Mankato schools. Norman and Edith Crooks, Amos and Rose Crooks, Glynn Crooks, and Amos Owen all participated.

1971 Norman and Edith Crooks led over sixty Dakota people on a walk to the hanging site to pay homage to the memory of the thirty-eight hanged warriors.

1971 Granite monument at hanging site removed.

1972 The first local "Reconciliation" Powwow in Mankato was held.

1978 The Mankato Mdewakanton Club (now the Mdewakanton Association) was established.

1978 A ceremony to honor the thirty-eight warriors hanged was initiated, conducted by Amos Owen on December 26th, the anniversary date of the hanging.

1980 A new marker of the location of the hanging site was dedicated by Dakota and Mankato City leaders.

1986 The annual Memorial Run from Fort Snelling to Mankato was initiated on

December 26th, the anniversary date of the hanging of the thirty-eight warriors.

1987 This year was declared "The Year of Reconciliation" by a proclamation of Governor Rudy Perpich.

1987 The first Education Day happened. Mankato schools bus more than a thousand school children and their teachers to the powwow grounds to visit learning stations presenting instruction about various American Indian arts and crafts and traditions.

1987 The *Winter Warrior* statue was dedicated on December 26th.

1989 The "Learning Center" was established at the powwow to provide visitors more opportunity to learn about American Indian (especially Dakota) culture.

1990 Amos Owen passed away on June 4 at age seventy-three in his home on the Prairie Island Reservation after a long battle with cancer.

1997 "Reconciliation Park" was dedicated September 21 in conjunction with the annual powwow.

References

Black Elk, *The Sacred Pipe* (Edited and recorded by Joseph Eppes Brown), University of Oklahoma Press, Norman, Oklahoma, 1953, 1959.

Boutin, Loren D., *Cut Nose: Who Stands on a Cloud*. North Star Press of St. Cloud, Inc., St Cloud, Minnesota, 2006.

Boutin, Loren D., *While God Was Hidden*, North Star Press of St. Cloud, Inc., St Cloud, Minnesota, 2008.

Churchill, Ward, *A Little Matter of Genocide: Holocaust and Denial in the Americas, 1492 to the present*. City Lights books, San Francisco, 1997, pp. 179-188.

Folwell, William W., *A History of Minnesota, Vol. II*, Minnesota Historical Society, St Paul, Minnesota, 1961, p.289.

Hughes, Thomas, *History of Blue Earth County*, Middle West Publishing Company, Chicago, Illinois, 1909.

Lerwi, Charles, "Frontier Fears: The Clash of Dakota and Whites in the Newspapers of Mankato, Minnesota, 1863-1865," *Minnesota Heritage*, Issue #5, January 2012, pp. 36-53.

Mails, Thomas E., *Mystic Warriors of the Plains*, Marlowe & Company, New York, 1995.

Oneroad, Amos E. and Skinner, Alanson B., *Being Dakota*, Anderson, Laura L., editor, Minnesota Historical Society Press, 2003.

Pond, Samuel W., *Dakota Life in the Upper Midwest*. Minnesota Historical Society Press, St Paul, Minnesota, 1986, p.81.

Trenerry, Walter N., *The Shooting of Little Crow: Heroism or Murder?* Minnesota History, 38: pp. 150-153.

Webster's New Twentieth Century Dictionary of the English Language, 2nd Ed., 1979.

Weekly Review, Mankato, Minnesota, April 27, 1886.

Weekly Review, Mankato, Minnesota, April 25, 1916.

Index

Including a List of Members and Associates of the Mdewakanton Association (often with no page numbers)

The author tried to get everyone listed and sincerely apologizes to anyone who was inadvertently omitted.

A powwow is much more than an event or conference. It is a conglomeration of social, commercial, spiritual, and recreational activities, and a very important part of a powwow is the people who make all the events happen. Over the (more than) forty years that the Mankato Powwow has been taking place, many people have been involved and have contributed to the success of the powwow, and this number continues to grow. Many people who were involved with the beginning of the powwow are still involved. Some have since passed away. What follows is a list of the people who have been, at one time or another, an important part of the powwow in Mankato.

Akisha (Hollerer), 46.

Aldinger, Marty. A long time member of the Mdewakanton Association, he and his wife, Debra Raiche, chaired the Gate Committee for about seven years. Together, with the help of other members of the Association, they collected two complete sets of powwow buttons. These sets were ceremoniously presented to Glynn and Stan Crooks of the Shakopee Sioux Community during the powwow at Mankato.

Alex, Terry. Was a member of the Mdewakanton Club for a short time.

Allen, Wayne and Colleen (Dakota). Taught flintknapping at a learning station on Education Day.

Amos Owen Parkette, 48, 49.

Anders, Betty and Brad. Were members of the Mdewakanton Club in 1991.

Anoka, Lou (American Indian). Taught beadwork at a learning station on Education Day.

Aubin, Darryl (Ojibwe) A long time member of the Mdewakanton Association, he has taken charge of the Grounds Committee in recent years, 86.

Aubin, Ray (Ojibwe) He was a member of the Mdewakanton Club when it was first chartered, and was one of the officers of the Club who signed the original charter, 86.

Bachmeyer, Sandy.

Baker, Sharynn. An Ojibwe member of the Lac Courte Oreilles tribe in Wisconsin, she was one of the vendors at the Mankato Powwow for many years, 110.

Baker, Vanessa (Dakota). Taught about jingle dress dancing and regalia at a learning station on Education Day.

Ballard, Conchita (Northern Cherokee). Mike's wife and one of the presenters at Education Day since the very beginning of this activity. She taught about children's games.

Ballard, Mike (Northern Cherokee). President of the Mdewakanton Club (1984 and 1985), Mike is always at the powwow and willing to help out with anything asked of him. On Education Day he had a station in which he taught about the games that Dakota children played, 61, 77.

Ballard, Roy Mike's son. Helped with setting up the powwow for some years.

Ballard, Sarah Jane. Mike's daughter who continues to help present games at Education Day.

Barry, Paul (Ute) Assumed the responsibility of directing the Education Day activities after the departure of Bruce and Sheryl Dowlin. He is also the main source for the Mdewakanton Association's website. On Education Day he teaches about tepee construction, 53, 54.

Barry, Vicki Paul's wife and main backer and an active member of the Mdewakanton Association, 53, 54.

Bassett, Bill. Mankato City Manager in 1980, he was very supportive of reconciliation efforts and the powwow. He was instrumental in the establishment of a new historical marker at the hanging site replacing the old stone marker that had been often vandalized, 26, 27, 49, 78.

Bateman, Jim. A Mdewakanton Club member who for years was the sound man at the bandstand and who contributed the use of his own equipment for some of those years.

Beaulieu (nee Blue) Sally (Dakota). Worked at the gate along with Vernell Wabasha at the first powwow in 1972, 24.

Becker, Richard. An Education Day resource person who passed away in 1988.

Bell, Doris (Ojibwe). American Indian who sold many buttons at the gate.

Benson, Ben (Mandan). He was on the faculty of Mankato State University and coordinated the school's powwow with the Mankato Powwow.

Berg, Ken As editor of the Mankato Free Press who wrote many editorials which were negatively slanted regarding any way of honoring the Dakota for their actions in the 1862 War. Still, he was in favor of reconciliation between the Dakota and the local white communities, 8.

Bergstrom, Gifford (Modoc). Was a member of the Mdewakanton Club for a time.

Beston, Julie (Dakota). Taught about the making of jingle dresses on Education Day.

Bieber, Duane. An early member of the Mdewakanton Club.

Bibeau, Herb (Ojibwe). Taught about men's dance regalia, dancing, Indian customs, and harvesting rice at an education station on Education Day, 62.

Bibeau, Marion (Seneca). Taught about women's dance regalia, dance, customs, and harvesting wild rice at an education station on Education Day.

Bienke, Erma. A very early and very active Club member, and instrumental in helping with the establishment of Education Day., 37, 60.

Bigaouette, Colleen. Was a member of the Mdewakanton Club in 1991.

Blackhawk, Barry. Was with Bud Lawrence on the first walk to Prairie Island in 1965. He also was one of the first presenters on Education Day, 16, 18, 118.

Blacksmith, Harold (Dakota). Taught about Dakota songs and the moccasin game at an education station on Education Day.

Blessing of the arena, 76.

Borneke, Don. At his own expense, he moved the uncut stone for the Winter Warrior to where it could be carved, and then he moved the finished statue to its final placement at the Mankato Library, 41.

Boutin, Beverly. Served as coordinator of the vendors at the powwow for several years and camped at the powwow for many more years. Old timers at the powwow still talk about the big jar of cookies that she always had available for visitors to her camp.

Boutin, Loren Dean. Served as President of the Mdewakanton Club in 1995 and 1996. Served as head of the Grounds crew for many years and continues to remain active with the powwow. Author of two books (Cut Nose and While God Was Hidden) which reflect, in part, some of his many experiences with the powwow.

Brady, John D. Past Mayor of Mankato, attended the powwow regularly and was a member of the Mdewakanton Club.

Brandenberg, Connie. Was a member of the Mdewakanton Club for a time.

Brave Heart, David (Dakota). Recently joined the Mdewakanton Association.

Broughton, Gene. Was a member of the Mdewakanton Club for a time.

Brushes, 109.

Brugman, Shirley. Was a member of the Mdewakanton Club for several years.

Buckley, James H. Sr. He walked from Mankato to Prairie Island with Bud Lawrence in 1969. One of the founders of the powwow, his leadership helped lay the groundwork for the first Mankato Powwow in 1972. He was an original charter member of the Mdewakanton Club. He was the Director of the Mankato YMCA at that time. Many of the planning meetings for the early Powwows were held in his office. He has continued to be very active with the powwow in subsequent years and can often be found working at the gate, vii, ix, 18-20, 22, 26, 27, 29, 39, 49, 54, 118.

Buckley, James Jr. Helped out at the powwow putting in many hours at the gate and various other activities.

Buckley, John. Helped out at the powwow putting in many hours at the gate and various other activities.

Buffalo Statue, 50.

Bullet proofing, 80.

Butz, Barbara Feezor-Stewart (Dakota). An anthropologist, she is a very assertive American Indian activist. She was a member of the Mdewakanton Club for a time. She also taught about foods and family organization on Education Day.

Callahan, Geri. A member of the Mdewakanton Club in 1991.

Campbell, Curtis (Dakota). Served on the Mdewakanton Advisory Committee.

Cansi' yapi Oyate Dance Group. Demonstrated dances at Education Day activities.

Carlstrom, George. A loyal supporter of the powwow, he contributed to it with many materials and in other ways, 37, 51.

Casper, Josh. Served as President of the Mdewakanton Club in 1999. He also worked Security and at First Aid.

Casper, Reta. Sam's wife and Josh's mother, Reta has been a long time member of the Mdewakanton Club.

Casper, Sam. Served as President of the Mdewakanton Club in 1997 and 1998. He has also been a vendor at the powwow.

Cavender, Chris. Served as Emcee at one of the early Powwows (1974). He read aloud the Governor's proclamation of the Year of Reconciliation at the first Memorial Run on December 26th, 1986, 43.

Ceremonies:
Adoption, 80.
Blessing of the Arena, 76.
Bullet Proofing, 80.
Condolences, 80.
Give Away, 79.
Grand Entry, 36, 68, 69, 83, 108, 110.
Healing, 76, 79-81.
Honor, 1, 45, 49, 68, 71, 78.
Naming, 1, 77.
Purification, 16, 44, 66, 96, 99.
Rain, 83, 84.
Remembrances, 1, 84.
Wedding, 79.

Christ, Stan. Former mayor of Mankato, he was a staunch supporter of the powwow during his tenure as mayor. He is suspected of being primarily responsible for the mysterious disappearance of the first monument to the thirty-eight. As mayor, he helped to get Reconciliation Park established in 1997, 9, 49.

Claridge, Merrill. Started out with Bud Lawrence and Jim Buckley on their walk to Prairie Island but stopped at Madison Lake, never intending to go the whole route, 19.

Clobes, Dave. A photographer with mixed blood who has been very active at the powwow.

Cook, Barb. A friend of the powwow and frequent donor to the Mdewakanton Club, she rarely misses a Mankato Powwow, 37.

Cook shack, 35, 46, 48, 84-86, 93, 106.

Commemorative Run, 43, 46.

Covey, Paul. Served on the Grounds crew and was a member of the Mdewakanton Club for a time, 33.

Crooks, Amos (Wambdi Hoksida, Eagle Boy) (Dakota). The first Tribal Chairman of the Shakopee Sioux Community, he was also one of the first supporters of the powwow in Mankato. He served as Emcee at the powwow in early years and in the 1980s. He was a long time member of the Club until he died in 1999. He also taught about traditional dancing on Education Day, 29, 67, 70, 110, 118.

Crooks, Edith (Dakota). Devoted wife of Norman, she contributed to the powwow in its earliest years and was a founding charter member, 29, 118.

Crooks, Glynn (Dakota). Made the Club's staff of thirty-eight eagle feathers representing the warriors who were executed. There were two more feathers on this staff representing chiefs Shakopee and Medicine Bottle who were hanged at a later time at Fort Snelling. This staff was carried to many communities to be an important representation of the powwow in Mankato, 37, 54, 118.

Crooks, Norman (Dakota). Was part of the group of American Indians who helped get the powwow established in 1972, and he remained a faithful supporter of the powwow until he died. He led a walk into Mankato on December 26 from north of town before the beginning of the Memorial Run, 27, 29, 54, 118.

Crooks, Rosemma (Dakota). Wife of Amos Crooks and mother of Glynn, she was very active in getting the powwow going, and she attended the powwow every year until she died in 2001. She also taught about traditional dancing on Education Day, 29, 54, 93, 94, 110, 118.

Crooks, Stan. Long time Tribal Chairman of the Shakopee Sioux Community, he has been very supportive of the Mankato powwow.

Croud, Jeanne Boutain (Ojibwe). On Education Day she taught about moccasin making.

Croud, Joe (Ojibwe) On Education Day he had a learning station in which he taught about American Indian flutes, 63.

Dakken, Dave. School District #77 Associate Superintendent who supported the Education Day project, 62.

Dances:
Basic step, 73.
Fancy Dance, 72, 73.
Grass Dance, 58, 70, 72.
Honor Dances, 49, 78.
Jingle Dress Dance, 59, 69, 72, 73.
Men's Traditional, 70.
Women's Fancy (Shawl) Dance, 73.
Women's Traditional, 71, 84.

Davenport, Bertha. Wife of Harvey, she and Harvey attended the first powwow and showed up annually at the powwow until Harvey died in 1994, 54.

Davenport, Harvey (Mesquakie). The first (and only) dancer on the first evening of the first powwow in 1972. He remained a faithful attendant, dancer, and vendor at the Mankato Powwow until he died in 1994, 24, 54, 81, 82.

Dearly, Jerry (Dakota). Served many times as Master of Ceremonies of the Mankato Powwow and has served in that capacity at many Powwows around the country. It is said that Jerry knows more about Powwows than any other man alive, 90, 113.

DeLeo, ReDeanna. A member of the Mdewakanton Club for a time.

DeLeo, Tony. A member of the Mdewakanton Club for a time.

Deloria, Vine Jr. (Lakota). Provided some of the impetus for initiating the Education Day project at the Mankato Powwow, 54, 59, 60.

Derby, Solomon. Served as Arena Director in 2011 and is continuing in that capacity and as a member of the Mdewakanton Association.

DeYonge, Alice. An important member of the Mdewakanton Club since 1992, she has been coordinator of volunteers for most of the past twenty years and an officer (Vice-Chair) of the Mdewakanton Association for the past

five years. In 2011 she is credited with "saving the powwow" because she did so much of the preparation for it.

Dierks, Lisa. Worked at the gate.

Dierks, Patric. Worked as a parking volunteer and cleanup after the powwow.

Dierks, Thorsten. Labored on the grounds crew.

Dow, John (Dakota). Taught about beadwork, pottery making, and the moccasin game on Education Day.

Dow, Melanie (Seneca). Taught about the moccasin game on Education Day.

Dowlin, Bruce. President of the Club (1986 and 1987). He provided much of the impetus for the initiation of the Commemorative Run on December 26, provided leadership for establishing Education Day at the powwow, was on the committee to establish the *Winter Warrior* and the buffalo memorial for the thirty-eight warriors hanged, 41, 43, 49, 55, 57, 79.

Dowlin, Sheryl. Her marriage to Bruce took place in a ceremony at the powwow. She has participated with Bruce in all of the activities listed above. She is considered to have spearheaded the Education Day project, 41, 49, 53, 54, 57, 59, 60, 79.

Drums, vii, 25, 54, 65-67, 83.

Duggan, Shirley. On Education Day she had a learning station at which she taught about American Indian ways of gathering food.

Eagles
As messengers of the Great Spirit, 70, 96.
As Spirits, 27, 28, 95, 110, 114.
At the first powwow 1972, 27.
When one dropped a feather, 96

Eastman, Emmett (Dakota). He served on the Mdewakanton Advisory Committee. A dancer at the powwow for many years, he is a marathon runner, very light on his feet, a pleasure to watch when he is dancing, and he led the runners in the Memorial Run for several years, 93.

Elfrink, Cheryl and Roger. Mdewakanton Club members in 1992, 101.

Engelby, Robert. A member of the Mdewakanton Club for a time.

Enjadi, Sharon. A member of the Mdewakanton Club for a time.

Enoch, Cody. Was the artist who designed the art for the poster and the programs of the Mankato Powwow.

Erickson, Guy. Served as President of the Club (1990). A former Army cook, he helped with many meals served by the Club. He organized a clothing drive for needy American Indians. He is now over ninety years old and continues to be active at the powwow, 47.

Fagin, Michael. As head of the Minority Groups Studies Center of Mankato State University, he brought groups of students to the Mankato powwow as part of their Diversity Program. He was listed as a member of the Mdewakanton Club for a time.

Feezor, Winifred (Dakota). On Education Day, she had a learning station where she taught about American Indian foods.

Felix, Butch Served as Emcee at the powwow for several recent years.

Ferris, Lydia (Dakota). Taught about Indian crafts on Education Day.

Finch, JoEllen. She and Joe Roy served together as President of the Mdewakanton Club (1980). Jo Ellen was one of the original Charter members.

Fisher, Richard A pipe carrier and one of the main fire tenders at the powwow and at the Spirit Fire for the Memorial Run on December 26th.

Flags, 34, 69, 76.

Fogel, Jerry. A concessionaire at the powwow who was willing to help Club members with any request made of him. He sold American Indian jewelry and always paid the full cost of three concession spaces.

Folson, Marlis. She prepared and served food for those who were resource persons on Education Day.

Founders, vii, 29, 31, 49, 93, 113.

Frazier, Brian (Santee Dakota). Taught about shield making on Education Day (2002).

Frazier, Cleo. A Resourse Person at Education Day.

Frazier, Jason (Dakota). New (2011) member of the Mdewakanton Association.

Frazier, Kermit (Santee Dakota). For many years he was a resource person on Education Day, teaching drum making, drumming/songs, leather work, hatchets, 62.

Frazier, Natasha (Santee Dakota). Taught about women's jingle dress at a learning station on Education Day.

Frazier, Raylone (Dakota). Taught about hide tanning on Education Day.

Frazier, Simon (Santee Dakota). On Education Day he had a learning station in which he taught about Dakota drums and songs.

Frazier, Vetal (Santee Dakota). On Education Day he had a station in which he taught about men's grass dance regalia.

Gale, Christina (Anishinabe or Ojibwe). Taught about women's jingle dress dance regalia and dancing at a learning station on Education Day.

Garlet, Diane. On Education Day she had a station in which she taught about beadwork and dream catchers.

Ganney, Anne. Was an active member of the Mdewakanton Club for a time and continues to contribute her time working at the "gate" very actively during the powwow.

Gau, Claire M. A member of the Mdewakanton Club in 1991.

Gerrish, Don. A new (2011) and enthusiastic member of the Mdewakanton Association.

Ghost Dancers, 106-109

Gilbert, Bill (Sisseton Dakota). A Great-great-grandson of Little Crow, he served as Arena Director in 1996. He was also on the Mdewakanton Advisory Committee. On Education Day he taught about the powwow, especially the opening ceremony, 96.

Give-away Ceremonies, 1, 79.

Godfrey, Ed (Dakota/Lakota). He was a dancer who served briefly as Emcee at the powwow, a Great-great grandson of Otakla (Many Kills), who was the one that Lincoln removed from the list of American Indians to be hanged. On Education Day he had a learning station in which he taught about the opening ceremony, the moccasin game, and gathering foods.

Godfrey, Shirley. On Education Day she taught about American Indian foods.

Goldtooth, Tom (Dine/Navaho). Was the powwow Arena Director from 1987 to 1990. He helped implement the initiation of the powwow's Education Day. He taught about the opening ceremony, culture, and the environment on Education Day, 56, 57.

Gouge, Lorraine (Dakota). Taught about Dakota culture at a learning station on Education Day.

Grand Entry, 36, 68, 69, 83, 108, 110.

Gray, John. For a number of years he was in charge of the volunteers and parking chores connected with the large number of cars that arrive at the powwow.

Gray, Jane (Vogel). Wife of John and a long time member of the Mdewakanton Club.

Hadley, Paul. He was able to see the importance of bringing the Sioux back into the community of Mankato and through his work as an Executive at the Mankato Chamber of Commerce he helped accomplish that.

Hall, Frank (Dakota from Sioux Valley, Canada). On Education Day he had a station in which he taught about the grass dance and regalia.

Hall, Solomon and Mary (Dakota from Sioux Valley, Canada). On Education Day they had a learning station in which they taught about tepee making, Dakota traditions, and Dakota culture.

Hamm, Ron. A new member (2010) of the Mdewakanton Association.

Hand, Floyd. Lakota medicine man, Amos Owen was his mentor as he learned his medicine. He was the Spiritual Leader at Amos' funeral.

Hanging, viii, 3, 4, 7, 8, 39-41, 43, 44, 50, 90, 98, 111, 112, 118, 119.

Hardie, Monine. A long time very active member of the Mdewakanton Club.

Hardt, Brad. President of the Mdewakanton Club (1992 and 1993). He was also Co-Chairman with Guy Erickson (1990) and with Marilyn Strasser (1992). He continues to be very active with the Club and always attends and participates in the powwow and the Memorial Run activities, 101, 104.

Hardt, Josh. Volunteered many hours working at the gate.

Hardt, Marilyn Felber. Brad's wife, she backed him in all his Club activities and was a member of the Mdewakanton Club for a number of years. Sho also participated in a women's walk to Prairie Island, 20.

Hasse, Arlo. Was a member of the Mdewakanton Club for a time.

Healer, 81, 82.

Hefner, Phil (Skip). Was a member of the Mdewakanton Club for a time.

Heminger, Roland. On Education Day he had a station in which he taught about Dakota drums and songs.

Heutmaker, Megan. New member of the Mdewakanton Association (2012) who immediately became Secretary of the Association.

Hiniker, Steve. He runs a local sawmill and for many years has donated firewood for the campers. He gives a reduced price and free delivery for the hardwood used at the Spirit fire for the sweat lodge, 96.

Honor Ceremonies, 45, 79.

Hornett, Charlie. Was a member of the Mdewakanton Club (1991).

Hotain, Mike (Dakota from Sioux Valley, Canada). Served the powwow as Emcee and also taught about Dakota culture, drumming, and songs on Education Day.

Howe, Travis. A relatively new member of the Mdewakanton Association (2010) who serves at the powwow as general handyman.

Howling Wolf, Jim. In 2010 he assumed the position of Vendor Coordinator for the Mdewakanton Association.

Iron Shield, Harold (Dakota). Served the powwow as Emcee.

Jeffers, Peg. A Principal at Hoover Elementary School who supported Education Day, 63.

Jefferson, Ed (Dakota). A member of the Prairie Island Counsel who helped with the mini powwow at the YMCA early on and was married to Amos Owen's niece, Barb, 18, 118.

Johnson, Jean. Wife of Les Johnson and a supporter of the Mdewakanton Club.

Johnson, Les ("Jeremiah"). Was Vice-president of the Mdewakanton Club when it first began in 1974. Later on, he spent many hours working with Amos Owen in the design of Land of Memories Park.

Kagermeier, Jeffrey. Was on the Committee to get the Reconciliation Park established in 1997, 49.

Kahnke, Rose. Was a member of the Mdewakanton Club and wrote her Doctoral thesis on the Mankato Powwow.

Keagy, Karla. Was a member of the Mdewakanton Club for a short time.

Klaus, Will (Dakota). On Education Day he taught about Dakota bead work and tepee construction. He was also an artist-vendor who sold mandellas (a mandella is a decorative wall hanging) and other American Indian crafts of his own making.

Klanderud, Bob (Dakota). The Akisha or "hollerer," also called "Bob The Cutter," 46.

Klein, Eva (Ojibwe). A very active member of the Mdewakanton Association for many years. In honor of her mother, she contributed a very nice and complete breakfast to campers, dancers, and all other comers at the powwow every year for about twenty years, 86.

Knights of the Forest, 4-7.

Konokowitz, Linda. A member of the Mdewakanton Club in 1991.

Kraay, Ron. Was a member of the Mdewakanton Club in 1991.

Kretch, Vicki. For several years she took charge of the feast preparation for the December 26th Memorial Run.

Kuhns, Geri. Was a member of the Mdewakanton Club in 1988.

Kunkel, Trudy & Lyle. Mdewakanton Club members in 1992.

LaBatte, John (Dakota). A local mixed blood American Indian who lives in New Ulm. He expressed an opinion that reconciliation is "impossible" between the Dakota and the local white communities, 113.

LaBatte, Walter ("Super") (Dakota). Served on the Mdewakanton Advisory Committee.

Lacher, Chris (Dakota). On Education Day he had a station in which he taught about tepee living.

Lame Deer, John Fire, 81, 82.

Land of Memories Park, 29, 30, 43-45, 47, 53, 56, 60, 93.

Larsen, Jayne. President of the Mdewakanton Club (1988 and 1989). Brought students from MSU to the powwow as part of the school's Diversity Program.

Larson, Big Dave (Dakota). Was a significant help in getting the powwow in 1972 started. He was one of the American Indians at that powwow who was recruited by Amos Owen. Served as Emcee at the powwow in early years, 29.

Larson, Dave (Dakota). He is "Big Dave's" son and one of the original presenters at Education Day. He is a past Tribal Chairman at the Lower Sioux Community. He recently served as Chairman of American Indian Affairs at Mankato State University. He is a well known speaker on American Indian history and culture. He has said, "For a long time when I came to Mankato it was with an uncomfortable feeling of false guilt. The first time I came to a powwow in Mankato I felt welcome, and it was like having that feeling of false guilt wiped away."

Larson, Karen. A member of the faculty at Gustavus Adolphus College in St Peter, she has been a member of the Mdewakanton Association for several years.

Lawrence, Al. He is the principal of Monroe School in Mankato and is the Student Coordinator of School District #77 who has managed the School District's end of Education Day activities in recent years.

Lawrence, Louis G ("Bud"). One of the three founders of the Mankato Powwow. An original charter member of the Mdewakanton Club, he served as President of the Club in 1972 and 1979 and again in 1994. He has been prominently involved in almost all of the reconciliation efforts that have taken place in the Mankato area including a clothing drive to help needy residents of the Prairie Island Reservation, instruction about American Indians in local schools, being one of the founders of the powwow, and establishing Reconciliation Park (the "Amos Owen Parkette") at the hanging site, vii, ix, 11, 12, 18, 19, 22, 24, 26, 29, 39, 41, 48, 49, 54, 81, 82, 86, 118.

LeBeau, Ellsworth (Lakota). He was in the Indian Affairs Department at Mankato State University and he was a member of the Mdewakanton Club for a time. On Education Day he taught about Dakota rituals and appropriate uses of tobacco.

LeClaire, Alice and Misty (Dakota). On Education Day they had a learning station in which they taught about women's dance regalia and the jingle dress.

Leith, Chris (Dakota). A Dakota medicine man, he was part of a mini powwow at the YMCA in early years and has conducted sweats at the Mankato Powwow, 18, 118.

Lichtenberg, Marian. A long time member of the Mdewakanton Club, she is always found working at the gate and she was the principal promoter of the local 5K Run to honor the thirty-eight. She was also an original member of the Club's Education Committee, 60.

Little Owl, Ralph (Mandan). With his wife Ida (Dakota) They were the only other American Indians, besides the Davenports, camping on site on Friday night at the first powwow in 1972. They camped in the outfield of the ballpark.

Lookinghorse, Arvol (Lakota). The nineteenth generation carrier of the white buffalo woman's sacred pipe, he brings his horse riders to the Memorial Run Ceremony on the anniversary of the hanging, 45.

Lundin, Vern. Former mayor of Mankato who had the inspiration for establishing Reconciliation Park, 39.

Mahoney, James.

Malebear, Willie (Dakota). Was instrumental (along with Bruce Dowlin) in initiating and establishing the Memorial Run on December 26th, 49.

Marsden, Rose. On Education Day she taught about the breastplates and chokers that the Dakota wore.

Martinka, Joe. Contributed use of the Kato Ballroom for a benefit dance in 1974, 25.

Max, Vincent (Dakota). Taught about the moccasin game at an education station on Education Day.

McCabe, Dennis. Was a member of the Mdewak-anton Club for several years in the 1980s, served as a general handyman, running a lot of errands, and as a person selling buttons at the gate.

McIntyre, Jackie. Was a member of the Mde-wakanton Club for a time.

McIntyre, Tom. Was a member of the Mde-wakanton Club for a time.

McGowan, Jack. A strong supporter of the pow-wow, he contributed a large tent for use at the powwow as shelter for the moccasin game. He also contributed a shelter for the volunteers at the powwow.

McMahan, Janet. Was in charge of the gate at the powwow for several years and a long time member of the Mdewakanton Club.

Mdewakanton Club (Association), vii, 29, 31-34, 36, 37, 41, 43, 45, 47, 53-55, 57, 59-61, 65, 77, 79, 84, 86, 87, 89, 91-93, 97, 99, 101, 114, 118.

Medicine man, 21, 80-82.

Melvin, Patty. Was a member of the Mdewakan-ton Club for a time.

Milano, Brenda. Was a member of the Mde-wakanton Club for a time.

Milda, Richard (Dakota). Served recently as Arena Director for several years, 95.

Miller, Marilyn. Was involved with Education Day and also worked at the gate selling buttons.

Miller, Thomas M. Sculptor of the *Winter War-rior* statue and the large buffalo at Reconcili-ation Park. The *Winter Warrior* statue was his own inspiration, 41, 49, 50.

Minnesota National Guard. Contributed the use of some tents and a field stove and helped set them up.

Mocal, Herb. Former Mayor of Mankato who was supportive of the powwow when the Land Of Memories Park was dedicated.

Mosca, Judy. Was a member of the Mdewakan-ton Club for a time.

Naming Ceremonies, 1, 77.

Nelson, Clyde R. (Bob). He was the K-12 Cur-riculum Director of School District #77 who gave the official go-ahead for Education Day at the Mankato Powwow in 1987, 54, 56.

Nolte, Dick. Was a member of the Mdewakan-ton Club for a time.

Nord, Kent. Taught about tepee construction on Education Day.

Oppel, Twylah. Was a member of the Mde-wakanton Club for a short time.

Ostland, Sharon. Supported the Mdewakanton Club with free ads in Home Magazine and with great advice to the Club regarding mar-keting and Direction.

Owen, Amos (Dakota). The only Indian among the three founders of the Mankato Powwow, he remained very active with the powwow until he died in 1990. He served the powwow in many capacities and in every way he could. He was also one of the original charter mem-bers of the Mdewakanton Club. He served at the powwow as Emcee in early years, traveled more than once to Europe to speak about rec-onciliation, and was Spiritual Leader at the powwow until he died, 11, 13-16, 18-20, 22-24, 26-30, 39, 41, 43, 47-54, 56, 57, 83, 97, 100, 101, 118.

Owen, Art (Dakota). He has been a long time member and participant at the powwow, was a key promoter of the Memorial Run and has served as Arena Director of the powwow. On Education Day he taught about traditional men's dancing regalia, 78, 103.

Owen, Ione (Dakota). The wife of Amos and mother of children Brenda, Arthur, Linda, Raymond, Mike, Clifford, and Duffy. Ione was one of the original charter members of the Mdewakanton Club and was a huge part of the work force at the powwow in early years, 53, 56, 57.

Owen, Linda (Dakota). Very active with the Mankato Powwow, she supervised the cook shack for several years.

Owen, Lisa. Ray's wife. She often worked hard at the cook shack.

Owen, Mike and Nick (Dakota). Mike was leader of the Prairie Island drum group. His drum often accompanies the runners on De-cember 26th. Mike and Nick together taught about traditional men's dance regalia and drumming and songs.

Owen, Ray (Dakota). Served as Spiritual Leader at the powwow and at the Memorial Run after his father's death in 1990. Ray was also one of the original charter members of the Mdewakan-ton Club. On Education Day, he taught about pipe making, drumming and songs, and ritual ceremoniesm, vii, ix, 102-104.

Owl as death messenger, 95.

Pearson, Maria (Dakota) (Running Moccasin). During early years of the powwow she was very influential in acquiring funding for the powwow. She also directed the production of many meals at the cook shack for several years. On Education Day she had a station in which she taught about story telling.

Pejuhutazizi Drum and Dance Group. "Pejuhutazizi" means "Yellow Medicine." On Education Day they had a learning station at which they taught dancing, drums/songs, and regalia.

Peters, Jerry (Dakota). An Education Day resource person who taught about Dakota culture and dance. He passed away in 1993.

Peterson, Jim "Scout." A college professor and "Mountain Man", he was as a member of the committee that established the Reconciliation Park. For many years he provided and set up a shelter for the Wabashas at the powwow, 49.

Petroff, Jim "Howling Wolf" (Dakota). Serves as the Vendor Coordinator at the powwow and member of the Mdewakanton Association since 2011.

Pettibone, Bruce (Dakota/Winnebago). Taught about beadwork at a learning station on Education Day.

Pipe Ceremonies, 43, 44.

Pittman, Deb and Eugene. Were members of the Mdewakanton Club for a short time.

Pratt, Allen (Dakota from the Sioux Valley Community in Canada). Actively participated in the Mankato Powwow. He was a resource person on Education Day and taught about Dakota culture and shields. He passed away in 1995.

Pullainen, Charles Son of Marilyn. Was a member of the Mdewakanton Club for a time.

Pullainen, Marilyn An early (since 1970s). Member of the Mdewakanton Club, she participated actively in Club meetings and preparations for the powwow and she attended the powwow faithfully even after her health began to fail her. She served as a special consultant to many Club members with regard to the "right way" for things to happen.

Purification ceremonies, 14, 44, 66, 96, 99.

Quick Bear, Tom ("the Healer"). In recent years he served in any capacity that he was asked to serve at the powwow. He had "healing powers" and would lay his hands on anyone with an affliction of any kind and pray for their reliefm, 82.

Raiche, Debra. Wife of Marty Aldinger. Together, they collected two complete sets of powwow buttons and coordinated activities at the gate for seven years.

Rain Ceremonies, 83.

Ray, Kenny (Dakota). A huge and very tough guy, Kenny served at the powwow as a Security person. Like most American Indians in attendance at the powwow, he would help out with just about anything when asked.

Reconciliation Park, 48-52, 119.

Reynolds, Keith. A close associate of Ray Owen. Keith has attended many powwows assisting Ray in every way possible, especially at the sweat lodge. He is a devotee of American Indian Spirituality, 101.

Rieman, Rodney. Was a member of the Mdewakanton Club for a time, and married Sarah Ballard.

Robb, Carie. She was an original charter member of the Mdewakanton Club and helped get the Club established in Mankato. She served as President of the Mdewakanton Club for two years (1977 and 1978), and she was Club Treasurer for six more years. Also, she made many powwow meals, 20, 25.

Robb, Donovan. Husband of Carie, He was active in helping to get the powwow started, 25.

Roberts, Floyd. As the Superintendent of the Parks Department of the City of Mankato, he was a strong supporter of the powwow.

Rojas, Ricardo. Was an early participant at the powwow and came to the powwow on horseback.

Rolfes, Bob. A workhorse for the Club year-round and especially at the powwow. He has been Club Treasurer for many years. He helped to get the powwow established from the very beginning. There are not enough words available to describe all that he has done for the Mdewakanton Club and how important he has been to the Club/Association, vii, 17, 118.

Ross, Diana. A Resource Person on Education Day (2002).

Roy, Joe. Was president of the Mdewakanton Club when it first began in 1974.

Roy, Richard. On Education Day he had a station in which he taught about moccasins.

Run: Mankato to Prairie Island (1965), (1969), 44-47, 77, 93, 118.

Running Wolf, Duane. Taught about winter count at a learning station on Education Day.

Rustad, Lyle A promoter who solicited funds for a movie about the powwow.

Scalp bounties, viii, 5-7, 74, 113.

Schrummer, Carrie (Dakota). Taught about Dakota legends and Dakota language at a learning station on Education day (2002).

Seaboy, Danny (Dakota). Served as emcee at the powwow for several years.

Seaboy, Londell (Dakota). Has served as Arena director of the powwow for two years.

Severin, Tom. Successor to Floyd Roberts as park superintendent, he has been a staunch supporter of the powwow.

Shoemaker, Dianne. Wife and companion to John.

Shoemaker, John. A spectator who, at every powwow, proudly wears all the buttons for all the powwows that have been held in Mankato, 92.

Schwartz, Bill. A member of the Mdewakanton Club, 1992

Siebrass, Hershel. President of the Mdewakanton Club (1983) A science teacher at West High School in Mankato. He is remembered for his favorite response to Vernell Wabasha when she would make a proposal for something new: "It's not in the budget." Still, he was a very strong force in promoting the powwow.

Sivanich, Mark. Was the first Treasurer for the powwow and was a very strong force in promoting the powwow. He is also remembered for his usual response to Vernell Wabasha when she wanted funds for something new: "It's not in the budget."

Smith, Emmett. Was a member of the Mdewakanton Club for a short time.

Smith, Louise Bluestone (Dakota). An Education Day resource person who taught about American Indian foods. She passed away in 1996.

Smith, Terry (Ojibwe). Was a vendor at the powwow who also served as a resource person on Education Day. He taught about traditional men's dance regalia.

Solyntjes, Chris. Long time member of the Mdewakanton Club and manager of the shirt concession, a fund raiser for the Club, at the powwow.

Songs, 45, 58, 65-68, 71, 72, 76, 102, 104.

Spirit Track, Ben Jr. (Yankton Sioux). Taught about dream catchers on Education Day (2002).

Stam, Candace. Was a member of the Mdewakanton Club for a time.

Stately, Romona. Coordinator for Education Day, 2011, 54.

Steiner, Pete. Hosted many Club members and members of the Dakota Community members to talk about the powwow on his radio talk show.

Steiner, Rod (Dakota). A vendor of American Indian artifacts and for many years he managed the vendors at the powwow as a member of the Mdewakanton Club.

Steiner, Shirley (Dakota). Rod's wife and very active in American Indian crafts.

Steinke, Inez. Was a member of the Mdewakanton Club for a time.

Stewart, Autumn (Dakota). Served as a resource person on Education Day.

Still Water Dancers. On Education Day they performed at an education station, demonstrating dancing, flute playing, and the LaCrosse game.

Strasser, Marilyn. Served as president of the Mdewakanton Club in 1990.

Stroud, Bridget. Was a member of the Mdewakanton Club for a time.

Strege, Jan. Was a member of the Mdewakanton Club for a time.

Sweat ceremony, 14, 15, 34, 44, 66, 86, 96-106.

Tacan, Kevin (Dakota, from Sioux Valley in Canada). Taught about the moccasin game on Education Day, 62.

Tacan, Marina (Dakota from Sioux Valley in Canada). Taught about star quilts and the Dakota language on Education Day.

Tallbear, Lee Ann (Dakota). A direct descendant of Chief Little Crow, she has been in charge of dancer registration for many years.

Taylor, Bill (Dakota from Sioux Valley in Canada, Eli's Grandson). He taught about dancing regalia on Education Day. He also initiated and conducted the moccasin game at the powwow in recent years.

Taylor, Eli (Dakota). A very aged Elder at the Sioux Valley Tribe in Manitoba, Canada, he attended the Mankato Powwow as an oral historian and story teller and participated as such on Education Day.

Tews, Wanda. One of the original charter members of the Mdewakanton Club.

Thomas, Larry. On Education Day he taught about drumming and songs.

Trudell, Roger (Santee Dakota). Served on the Mdewakanton Advisory Committee and is a drummer and singer on the Mazekute Drum Group that is often the host drum at the Mankato Powwow. At the time of this writing he is the Tribal Chairman of the Santee Community, 62.

Turner, Andrea "Scout." Was a member of the Association and everyone's gofer for a few years.

Urick, Fred (Dakota). Loved to dance and he was also a participant in Education Day activities. He also volunteered to help with many powwow related tasks.

Utzinger, Rollie. An administrator at School District #77 who helped facilitate Education Day.

Van Voorhis, Mary. President of the Mdewakanton Club (1981). She cooked buffalo burgers for sale at the powwow as a fund raiser for the Mdewakanton Club.

Vendors, ix, 24, 28, 30, 31, 34-36, 89-91, 106.

Voda, Charlie and Teresa. Were members of the Mdewakanton Club for a time.

Wabasha, Ernie (Dakota). An original charter member of the Mdewakanton Club, He is the Hereditary Chief of the Mdewakanton tribe. He was at the powwow in 1972 and, despite severe physical debility, he has attended all of the powwows since then and was available to anyone who wanted to meet and talk with him. He has also been a member of the Mdewakanton Advisory Committee, 16, 29, 39, 49, 54.

Wabasha, Leonard (Dakota). Has served as president of the Mdewakanton Association several years recently and has been a dancer and part of the powwow for most of his life. He also has served as a member of the Mdewakanton Advisory Committee. He now carries the Wabasha family staff in powwows, vii, 95.

Wabasha, Vernell (Dakota) She was an original member of the Mdewakanton Club. She was in charge of the gate at the first powwow in 1972 and has been the money manager and in charge of almost everything at every powwow ever since. On Education Day she had a learning station in which she taught about Dakota pottery, 9, 10, 16, 24, 29, 39, 49, 50, 54, 109.

Walker, Jeff. Was a member of the Mdewakanton Club for a time.

Waltman, Ed. Superintendent at School District #77 who helped facilitate Education Day and was otherwise a strong supporter of the powwow.

Wandersee, Gene. Was a member of the Mdewakanton Club for a time.

Wacipi, 21, 65, 76.

Wasicuna, Glen (Dakota from Sioux Valley in Canada). Taught about Dakota Culture and language on Education Day.

Wasicuna, Glenn. Was elected Co-Vicechairman of the Mdewakanton Association in 2006, sharing that position with Art Owen.

Wedding ceremonies, 79.

Wells, Gertrude. She was an original charter member of the Mdewakanton Club. Her closest friends called her "Pudge". She was part of the group of American Indians who helped get the powwow going in 1972. She remained active with the powwow until she passed away, 19, 29, 95.

Wells, Roger (Dakota). Served as resource person on Education Day.

Wells, Wallace H. (Wally). He was an original charter member of the Mdewakanton Club. He contributed significantly to the planning and production of the first powwow in 1972. He was Bud Lawrence's initial link to Amos Owen, 12, 18, 19, 29, 118.

Wesaw, Colin (Potawatomi/Mohawk). Taught about story telling on Education Day, 61.

Wethorne, Deanna. A Resource Person on Education Day.

Whipple, Babe (Santee Dakota). On Education Day he had a learning station where he taught about shields, tepee lamps, and graphic designs.

Whipple, Buddy (Dakota). Assembled the Club's first Advisory Committee, Chaired the Committee, was a resource person for Education Day, strongly supported the Club for many years until his passing in 1995.

Whipple, Dottie (Dakota). On Education Day she had a learning station at which she taught about traditional dance regalia and kinship and family roles, 62.

Whipple, Harlan (Dakota). Taught about Dakota ceremonial tobacco on Education Day, 62.

White, Porky (Ojibwe). Served as emcee at the powwow. He was also a Spiritual Leader for the Anishinabe Indians, 83.

Whitinger, Leila. Was a member of the Mdewakanton Club for a time.

Wiebold, LeRoy. Blue Earth County sheriff who actually deputized some of the Mdewakanton Club members to serve as security at the powwow.

Williams, Maude (Dakota). On Education Day she taught about drying corn and preparing corn soup.

Willis, Jean. Was a member of the Mdewakanton Club for a short time.

Wilson, Errin (Dakota). In 2011 assumed the position of Treasurer for the Mdewakanton Association.

Wilson, F. Joseph. Was a member of the Mdewakanton Club for a time.

Winter Warrior, 41, 50, 56, 119.

Wolfchild, Sheldon (Dakota). A talented actor and sculptor, he supported the Mankato Powwow while he was Chairman of the Lower Sioux Tribal Council. He was also instrumental in getting the horse ride from South Dakota started for the December 26th ceremony, 9.

Wolke, Arlene. Now deceased, she was for many years the coordinator of the concessions at the powwow.

Wolke, Tom. Helped Arlene and did work on the Grounds crew as well.

Wood, Pam. Was a member of the Mdewakanton Association in 2006.

Wood, Perry. One of the founders of Reconciliation Park, 49.

Wright, Phillip (Dakota). Had a learning station on Education Day at which he taught about Dakota culture. He also was a respected elder at the Lower Sioux Reservation who often gave impromptu speeches at the powwow.

Wyatt, Thomas. Taught about drumming and singing on Education Day.

Zeidler, Bob. Was a member of the Mdewakanton Club for a time.

Zielski, Dan. Spearheaded the production of a compact disc recording of the drumming and singing and verbal presentations at the powwow. Dan has been a dedicated member of the Mdewakanton Association for many years. He is also a devoted believer in American Indian Spirituality and often attends the Purification Ceremony at Prairie Island on Fridays traveling a great distance to do so.

Zoet, Bob. Active in a canoe club in Mankato, he arranged for a very long voyagers' canoe to be brought to the powwow and gave visitors rides in it on the Minnesota River.

Zwickey, Jim. President of the Mdewakanton Club even before there was a club (1974-1976). The Club became chartered under his leadership.

Acknowledgements

This book was the inspiration of Bud Lawrence and Jim Buckley, who with the late Amos Owen, are called "founders" of the Mankato Powwow. They provided much of the material and many of the records researched in the writing of this book, and they were readily available consultants whenever questions would arise. Along with Amos Owen, Jim and Bud will be long remembered for their tireless work at the powwow. If any two people could have finished the work of reconciling the two sides of the 1862 War, they would have done it.

I am also very appreciative of the steady support and encouragement of my friends Ed Red Owl and Michael Selvage who are always quick to respond to whatever I ask of them.

My writer's group (John Hurd, Nannette Rushton, Lorna Rafsness, Joan Brown, and Jackie Hilgert) was patient with my readings and gave good constructive criticisms.

My wife, Bev, was my chief editor, fierce critic, and best friend in this effort.

Thanks also to my cat, "Scamper," who was my constant companion through all the effort of this work. I was never alone.

Bruce and Sheryl Dowlin worked closely with me to co-write the material about Education Day and validate the history of that event and their cooperation was appreciated.

I needed authentication and validation of my work from the Dakota who were affiliated with the powwow. That was provided to some extent by Vernell Wabasha, Ed Red Owl, and Michael Selvage, Roger Trudell, Jerry Dearly, and Dave Larson.

My thanks also goes to Terry Morrow and Charles Lewis for their help regarding scapling laws.